Shakespeare MADE IN CANADA

Shakespeare
MADE IN CANADA

Contemporary Canadian Adaptations
in Theatre, Pop Media and Visual Arts

Edited by Daniel Fischlin & Judith Nasby

MACDONALD STEWART ART CENTRE

[Shakespeare] is a savage who had
some imagination. He has written
many good lines—but his pieces can
please only at London and in Canada.

—*Voltaire*

Contents

Dedication

I AM DELIGHTED to serve as the Honorary Chair of the Shakespeare—Made in Canada festival and to join with Guelph-Wellington and the University of Guelph in celebrating Shakespeare!

The festival, a true collaboration among different community members, will put Canada in the international spotlight by exhibiting the Sanders portrait, the Canadian portrait of Shakespeare. As well, the schedule of events—performances of drama, music, and spoken word; museum and educational exhibitions including a wide variety of visual arts—will attract more than 60,000 students, families, arts patrons, and academics from this region and far beyond. I know of no other group of individuals and organizations that has taken on a project of this magnitude. To focus the artistic talents of the community and region on a celebration of Shakespeare is truly phenomenal.

From my years in the theatre, I have come to learn that each of us builds our own relationship with Shakespeare and that his messages, after four hundred years, still resonate with us, as individuals and as communities. I encourage you to enjoy this exhibition and to attend many of the tremendous performances and activities that are a part of the festival!

Yours sincerely,
William Hutt
Honorary Chair, Shakespeare—Made in Canada Festival

Foreword

IT GIVES ME TREMENDOUS pleasure to welcome you to Shakespeare—
Made in Canada, a unique and dazzling exhibition and celebration of
history, culture, and country.

You will have the opportunity to view traditional and contemporary
art, learn about theatre design, test your knowledge of the Bard, see
authentic costumes and rare works from theatre archives, take a turn
at centre stage, and even try out a most modern Shakespearean adaptation: a state-of-the-art video game. Along the way, you'll learn how
the most produced playwright in history has influenced Canada's artists, writers, actors, and scholars, and, in the process, Canada's evolving
sense of itself as a nation. At the centre of this spectacle is the Sanders
portrait of William Shakespeare, widely thought to be the only image
of the Bard painted while he was alive. This magnificent painting is believed to depict Shakespeare at age thirty-nine and is matched in drama
only by the tale of its discovery.

The portrait was held in Canadian Lloyd Sullivan's family for some
four hundred years and, at one time, was stored under his grandmother's bed. It is believed that Shakespeare sat for an ancestor of Sullivan's,
an actor and painter called John Sanders, in 1603. You will discover how
this painting came to be connected to the University of Guelph. Suffice
it to say, it is a wonderful example of the important role of universities
and scholarly research in uncovering national treasures.

Indeed, this entire exhibition is illustrative of the many ways Canadian scholarship helps provide the necessary social, historical, economic, religious, and archival contexts for better understanding the past and exploring our futures. It is also a way for us to showcase the cultural excellence of our city and our region, from theatre and music to other educational programs and events, and to highlight the importance of the relationship we share with our community.

By working together, we have created a regional cultural synergy that allows us to produce collaborations such as Shakespeare—Made in Canada. So open your eyes and your minds and feast on the visual and intellectual treasures that await you inside this uniquely Canadian exhibition.

Alastair J. S. Summerlee
President and Vice-Chancellor
University of Guelph

Preface

SHAKESPEARE—MADE IN CANADA is a collaborative effort spearheaded by the City of Guelph, Guelph Arts Council, Macdonald Stewart Art Centre, Stratford Festival, and the University of Guelph. It began as an idea late in 2004 and has since blossomed to involve more than thirty-five local arts and cultural organizations in the development of a festival that will run from January to May 2007.

The origin of this festival, quite simply, was the opportunity to borrow the Sanders portrait of Shakespeare. The tale of how the portrait came to Guelph needs to be recorded on these pages as a testament to the strength of friendship and the value of scholarly research to Canadian society.

After seeing the Sanders portrait at the Art Gallery of Ontario in 2001, Daniel Fischlin, professor in the School of English and Theatre Studies at the University of Guelph, got the idea of featuring the portrait as the signature image on the University's Canadian Adaptations of Shakespeare Project (CASP) website <www.canadianshakespeares.ca>. The site, created by Fischlin and a team of graduate and undergraduate students, is the largest and most complete in the world dedicated to showing the playwright's cultural influence on Canada. Fischlin approached portrait owner Lloyd Sullivan of Ottawa, a retired Bell engineer, who had been for many years single-handedly and painstakingly researching the provenance of the portrait. Sullivan agreed to the use of the portrait on the CASP website, and a fast friendship between Sullivan and Fischlin developed. As it happened, they discovered that they shared the same experience of growing up and being educated in Montreal. They even attended the same elementary and secondary schools, the Daniel O'Connell School, run by the Irish Christian Brothers, and Loyola High School, run by the Jesuits.

The idea of bringing the Sanders portrait to the University of Guelph and featuring it as the focal point of a Canadian festival devoted to the works of Shakespeare started as a suggestion made at a luncheon meeting attended by Sullivan, Fischlin, Alastair Summerlee, president and vice-chancellor of the University of Guelph, and Joanne Shoveller, vice-president, Alumni Affairs and Development, in Ottawa on November 19, 2004. The loan of the portrait was later arranged; its display at the University of Guelph will be only the third time in its history that it has been shown in public.

Realizing that there was an opportunity to reach out into the community to join together to create a series of events around the exhibition of the portrait, Summerlee suggested that the City of Guelph, Guelph Arts Council, Macdonald Stewart Art Centre, and Stratford Festival be approached to become partners. Two major thrusts were established. A curatorial team, lead by Judith Nasby, director and curator of the Macdonald Stewart Art Centre, developed the idea of an expansive exhibition to present contemporary Canadian adaptations of Shakespeare in theatre, pop media, and visual art as a complement to the Sanders portrait. The Canadian Adaptations of Shakespeare Project, Macdonald Stewart Art Centre, Office of Open Learning, School of English and Theatre Studies, Stratford Festival, and Guelph's L. W. Conolly Theatre Archives all agreed to participate in the development of the exhibition. The City of Guelph, Guelph Arts Council, and University of Guelph agreed to support the development of a region-wide festival of activities focusing on Shakespeare and community partnerships.

A call to the regional arts and cultural community went out in September 2005. Ninety groups were sent an invitation to a meeting to discuss the viability of hosting a region-wide festival around an exhibition of the Sanders portrait. More than sixty people representing forty-five arts and cultural organizations attended. There was tremendous enthusiasm expressed at the meeting; from it came a community-based volunteer organizing committee that directed the development of the Shakespeare—Made in Canada festival and its activities.

Later that fall, a call for expressions of interest went out to artists and cultural volunteers who were asked to submit ideas for performances (music, dance, drama, and so forth), visual arts, and exhibitions that would share the theme of Shakespeare. By February 2006, more than thirty groups had submitted ideas and the activities were slotted into an exciting and exhaustive program for the festival.

The idea for the exhibition and festival gathered further momentum. In the spring of 2006, the University of Guelph garnered one of the most coveted prizes in the history of theatre in Canada. William Hutt, Canada's most prominent and experienced classical Shakespearean actor, donated his papers to the L. W. Conolly Theatre Archives. As a vocal advocate for the development of a uniquely Canadian theatre tradition, Hutt was immediately engaged by the notion of Shakespeare—Made in Canada, and agreed to become the honorary chair of the festival.

No tale is complete without including its intricate twists and turns of human passion. Of all places, Hutt was to find his perfect foil in the Astrophysics Laboratory at the University of Guelph. Diane Nalini de Kerckhove, a renowned academic, had recently joined the faculty. To the surprise of many, her excellence in research and teaching was mirrored in her talent as a jazz singer and songwriter. As fate would have it, she was about to release her third CD, *Diane Nalini: Songs of Sweet Fire,* the songs and sonnets of William Shakespeare. Learning of Shakespeare—Made in Canada and of Hutt's patronage, Nalini offered to launch the CD to promote the festival. In May 2006, Shakespeare—Made in Canada was officially launched with a live performance by Nalini, hosted by Hutt, which attracted national attention from across the arts and entertainment sector.

By the fall of 2006, more than thirty-five organizations from across the Guelph-Wellington region had committed to making Shakespeare—Made in Canada a festival of local, regional, national, and international significance.

The groundswell of commitment to this project has attracted the support of local business leaders, government, and public officials. Their enthusiasm and dedication to this project establishes a benchmark in excellence in community cooperation for which we are all truly indebted. I am grateful for the opportunity provided to me by President Summerlee and the University of Guelph to become involved in such a great project. I offer my humble and heartfelt thanks to all of those who have contributed to the success of Shakespeare—Made in Canada.

Sue Bennett
Director, University and Community Relations
Project Manager, Shakespeare—Made in Canada festival
University of Guelph

Introduction to the
Education Program

OFFICE OF OPEN LEARNING is pleased to be a contributing partner, bridging the University of Guelph's teaching and research expertise with the Shakespeare—Made in Canada initiative. The festival is an example of how successful collaboration among communities can provide enriching cultural experiences, while highlighting our region and its people.

Shakespeare—Made in Canada brings together a wide range of rich resources that represent the extent to which the Bard has influenced Canadian culture and society. The cornerstone of the exhibition, the Sanders portrait and its journey, stokes the fires of imagination. We have translated this into the development and delivery of an interactive educational program for elementary and secondary students. Programming and school tours focus students on the growth and refinement of knowledge and skills in the visual arts, English, drama, history, and science, through Canadian adaptations of Shakespeare.

Our sincere thanks to the Upper Grand District School Board and the Wellington Catholic District School Board for their partnership in the development of the school education program. Curriculum consultants from our local school boards have made invaluable cross-curricular connections that enhance students' learning and their application of knowledge and understanding.

In addition, our appreciation to those involved with the Canadian Adaptations of Shakespeare Project and the Macdonald Stewart Art Centre for their leadership in this unique exhibition.

Enjoy this cultural celebration and experience the mystery and magic of Shakespeare.

Virginia L. Gray
Director, Office of Open Learning
University of Guelph

Acknowledgments

WE WISH TO THANK the many individuals and organizations who have made the exhibition Shakespeare—Made in Canada: Contemporary Canadian Adaptations in Theatre, Pop Media, and Visual Arts possible.

We thank University of Guelph President Alastair Summerlee for his enthusiasm and vision in initiating the exhibition—few university presidents have committed so wholeheartedly to such a large-scale undertaking for the arts.

We thank Sue Bennett, Director of University and Community Relations, for her extraordinary tenacity, drive, and imagination in laying the logistical groundwork as Project Manager of the Shakespeare—Made in Canada festival.

We thank our team of co-curators who worked together so effectively, bringing forward new research, as well as fascinating and rare objects: Lorne Bruce, Head of Archival and Special Collections, University of Guelph Library; Jane Edmonds, Archivist and Researcher, Stratford Festival; Pat Flood, Professor, School of English and Theatre Studies, University of Guelph; Jim Hunt, Professor Emeritus, Department of Physics, University of Guelph; and Leanore Lieblein, former Associate Professor and Chair, English Department, McGill University. We are proud to be publishing their engaging curatorial and critical writing, a lasting document of our collaboration in theatre, pop media, and visual arts. This book also contains written contributions by Pat Morden, in association with the Stratford Festival of Canada, and Lorna Rourke, Liaison Librarian, University of Guelph.

The education program was developed and coordinated by the Office of Open Learning at the University of Guelph through the dedication of Virginia L. Gray, Director; Petra Schennach, Senior Continuing Education Manager, Program Development; and Richard Louttet, Program Manager. The education program engages regional elementary and secondary school students with Shakespeare through hands-on artistic, dramatic, and scientific modules. We thank Diane Nalini de Kerckhove, Assistant Professor, Department of Physics, for her valuable contributions to the program.

We pay special tribute to Lloyd Sullivan, owner of the Sanders portrait, for his thought-provoking essay and the incredible generosity he has given over the two years it has taken to research and organize this exhibition.

We acknowledge the support of, among many others, the following individuals for their contributions to this complex undertaking: Jennifer Ailles, Claire Alexander, Kim Anderson, Hanna Armoceta, Lynne Armstrong, Rosemarie Armstrong, Luis Artagnan, Mary Aski-Piyesiwiskwew Longman, Jean Asselin, Jane Baldwin, Sharon Ballantyne, Aimee Barber, Lori Barnsley, Michael Barnstijn, Bill Barrett, Kate Barris, Micheline Beaulicu, Larry Beckwith, Sue Bennett, Darren Berberick, David Bevington, John Bligh and Nancy Bailey Bligh, Pierrette Boisvert, Charles Bolster, Lori Bona Hunt, Chris Boyadjian, Susan Bozic, Robert C. Brandeis, Michael Braudo, Mr. and Mrs. Doug Bridge, Paul Brigg, Daniel Brooks, Donald Bruce, Diana Brydon, Marie Buntin, Ross Butler, Lynn Campbell, Vince Campolongo, Clifford Cardinal, Rod Carley, Michelle Chanonat, Cathy Chaput, Ellen Charendoff, Gabriel Charpentier, Neil Cheney, William Chesney, Antoni Cimolino, Patrick Clark, Chris Coculuzzi, Ben Coe, Josée Comtois, Jaclyn Conley, Rachelle Cooper, Joanne Coyle, Nick Craine, Bob Creedy, Chuck Cunningham, Mathew Currelly, Oliver Cutz, Richard Dankert, Oswaldo DeLeón Kantule, Paula de Vasconcelos, Doreen D'eath, Charlotte Dean, Richard and Jane Dell, Michael Denny, Pierre Desjardins, Kendra Dewar, Mary Dickieson, Jennifer Drouin, Gilbert Duclos, Ben Dugas, Eugènie Dumais, Brad Eccles, Jane Edmonds, Bill and Elizabeth Edwards, Tibor Egervari, Kathryn Elton, Lars Eriksson and Mary-Jane Preston, Robert

Etcheverry, Karen Farbridge, Elizabeth Farrell, FASTWÜRMS, Marjorie
Fielding, Dorothy Fisher, Elie Flynn Quartet, Waawaate Fobister,
Mark Fortier, Peter Freund, Anita Gaffney, David Gardner, David
Garneau, Michel Garneau, Sky Gilbert, Herminia Gillingham, Sharon
Godwin, Jeffrey Golde, Tanya Gough, John Graham, Ken Graham,
Kathe Gray, Carl Griffin, Darina Griffin, Scott Griffin, Marion Gruner,
Hugh Guthrie, Aubrey Hagar, Jim Hale Sanders, Ken Hammill, Bob
Hammond, Kathy Hanneson, Dave Harnden, Verne Harrison, John
Harrod, Andrew Harwood, Drew Hayden Taylor, Pam Healey, Anne
Henderson, the Holody family, Ken Hudson, Jim Hunt, William Hutt,
Ron Ingle, Robert Ireland, Erika A. Iserhoff, Sujata Iyengar, Hal and
Nancy Jackson, Bill and Sue Jaine, Astrid Janson, Falen Johnson, Dr.
and Mrs. L. Jones, Michael Keefer, John Kelly Cuthbertson, Kevin
Kemp, Daniel Kieffer, Tom King, Fiona Kinsella, Emanuelle Kirouac-
Sanche, John Kissick, Caroline Knight, Susan Knight, Peter Kucharski,
Raymond Lafontaine, Harry Lane, Lyne Lapointe, Roland Laroche,
Craig Lauzon, Jani Lauzon, Marcie Lawrence, Darryl Leeson and Chris
Montgomery, Danielle Léger, Marc l'Espérance, Gordon Lester, Danièle
Lévesque, Stephen Livick, Art Lucs, Sandra Lucs, Dany Lyne, Louise
MacCallum, John MacDonald, Brian MacFarlane and Christa Bisantz,
Rob MacKay, Kennedy (Cathy) MacKinnon, Sue Ann Maharaj, Irena
Makaryk, Maureen Mancuso, Marion Manning, Lee Maracle, Cheri
Maracle-Cardinal, Wayne Marsh, Deborah Maskens, Dawn Matheson,
Maureen Maxwell, Mark McCutcheon, Heather McDonald, Gail
McGinnis, Marissa McHugh, Drew McIvor, Ann Melnyk, Lewis Melville,
John and Deborah Mercer, Jean-Guy Methot and Peggy Humston,
Jackson Mill, Jaime Mishibinijima, Monique Mojica, Sorouja Moll,
Richard Monette, Ian Montagnes and Elizabeth Wilson, Don Moore,
Jennifer Moore, Brian Morel, Sue Morrison, David Murray, Deborah
Murray, Jacqueline Murray, Martha Nandorfy, Bill Nelson, Anthony
Newman, Gregmar Newman, Shelley Niro, Ginette Noiseux, Renée
Noiseux-Gurik, Yvette Nolan, Paul Ord, France Ouellette, Dean Palmer,
Milt and Sandra Parcher, Evan Penny, Brian Pettigrew, William R. and
Sydney Pieschel, Ryan Price, David Prosser, Kate Quarrie, Pat Quigley,
Andrew Reid, Yves Renaud, Phyllis Reynen, Shannon Reynolds, Michael
Ridley, Sandra Roberts, Ryan Robertson, Stuart Robertson, Richard Rose,
Larry Rossignol, Jean-Louis Roux, Gerry Rubio (in memoriam), Mary

Rubio, Cheryl Ruddock, Will and Jenny Ryan, Sandy Sabatini, Helen Salmon, Paul Salmon, Denis Salter, Chris and Charlene Sanderson, John Satterberg and Nina Keogh, Andrew Saunders, Christine Schindler, Djanet Sears, Richard Séguin, Skip Shand, Alan Sharpe, Alan Shepard, Joanne Shoveller, Sara Sinclair, Barbara Singer, Arline Smith, Bettina C. Smith, Hanna Smith, Mary-Anne Sodonis, Kathryn Ssedoga, Donna Michelle St. Bernard, Michelle St. John, Hélène M. Stevenson, Nick Storring, Lloyd and Mary Sullivan, Nancy Sullivan, Adam Symansky, Paul-Antoine Taillefer, Judith Thompson, Helen Thundercloud, Douglas W. Todd, Jean-Paul Tousignant, Sue Trerise, Sue Turmel, Shawn Turner, Chris Vandergrift, Margaret Vanderwoude, Ben Walsh, Janet Wardlaw, Michaela Washburn, Bill Whitehead, Herbert Whittaker (in memoriam), Alan Wildeman, Neil Williamson, Ann Wilson, Pierre Wilson, William Winegard, Sally Wismer, Yvonne Yates, Sean Yo, and Abebe Zezewo Peters.

Shakespeare—Made in Canada would not have been possible without the generous support of the following organizations: A. K. Collings Gallery (Port Hope), Aboriginal Resource Centre, Apple Canada, Arcady Films, Art Gallery of Northumberland, Art Gallery of Ontario, Assante Wealth Management, Association for Canadian Theatre Research, Balnar Management Ltd., Bank of Montreal, Barry Cullen Chevrolet Cadillac, Barzotti Woodworking Ltd., Bibliothèque et Archives Nationales du Québec, Canada Council for the Arts, Canadian Conservation Institute, Canadian Opera Company, Canadian Theatre Review, Canstage, City of Guelph, College of Arts at the University of Guelph, Datamatrix, Dr. Lawrence Jones & Associates Dentistry, E. J. Pratt Library at Victoria University (University of Toronto), Edward Johnson Public School (2005–2006 Grade 6 class), electric pear, Ex Machina, Framing & Art Centre (Guelph), Folger Shakespeare Library, Form & Function Cabinetmakers (Port Hope), Guelph Arts Council, Guelph Mercury, Guelph Tool, Guelph Wellington Men's Club, Hammond Power Solutions, Helen Gardiner Phelan Playhouse, John Sutherland & Sons Limited, L. W. Conolly Theatre Archives at the University of Guclph, Library and Archives Canada, Lift Technologies, Linamar, M&T Printing Group at the University of Guelph, McCord Museum of Canadian History, McDonald's, Montreal Museum of Fine Arts, Musagetes Fund at the Guelph Community Foundation, Musée des Maîtres et Artisans du Québec, National Film Board of Canada, National Theatre School of

Canada, Native Earth Performing Arts, Necessary Angel Theatre Company, Office of Open Learning at the University of Guelph, Office of the President at University of Guelph, Old Quebec Street Shoppes & Office Suites, Ontario Arts Council, Pheonix Community Works Foundation (Toronto), Pigeon Collective, Premier's Research Excellence Awards, Price Waterhouse Coopers, Productions Jean-Pier Doucet, Red Car Service, River Run Centre, Robinson Pontiac GMC Buick Ltd., RONA, Rotary Club of Guelph, Rotary Club of Guelph Charitable Foundation, Royal LePage Royal City Realty, Schneider National Carriers, School of English and Theatre Studies at the University of Guelph, Shakespeare Arms, Sleeman All Natural Ales & Lagers, Social Sciences and Humanities Research Council of Canada, St. John's-Kilmarnock School, Stratford Festival of Canada, Stratford Theatre, Swan Moving and Storage, TD Canada Trust, Tarragon Theatre, Technovision Interactive Inc., Théâtre du Nouveau Monde, Théâtre Espace Go, Theatre Museum Canada, Théâtre Omnibus, Théâtre Ondinnok, The Co-operators, Therapy Partners, Thunder Bay Art Gallery, Toronto Masque Theatre, Upper Grand District School Board, Valcom, Vilnis Design Works, Wall-Custance Funeral Home Ltd., Wayne Pitman Ford Lincoln Inc., Weiler & Company Chartered Accountants, Wellington Catholic District School Board, Wellington Motors, Zellers, and Zehrs.

We appreciate the creativity, hard work, good will, and professionalism of our staff who helped prepare the exhibition. From the Canadian Adaptations of Shakespeare Project, we thank Mat Buntin, Project Manager, and from Macdonald Stewart Art Centre we thank Verne Harrison, Gallery Coordinator; Sorouja Moll, Administrative Assistant; Dawn Owen, Assistant Curator; Aidan Ware, Public Programming Assistant; and Don Russell, Installation Assistant. We also thank our part-time employees and academic interns: Rachel Albano, Chris Beard, Miranda Bouchard, Blair Brandon, Amanda Brason, Laura Bydlowska, Myles Calvert, Joshua Clemenson, Jennifer Cupid, Emily Drinkwater, Joel Fullerton, Seth Gerry, Justin Gould, Katherine Hanz, Nicole Hewat, Sabrina Hope, Rachelle Kelly, Alison Little, Pam Lobb, Alissa Lumsden, Eileen MacArthur, John Mattucci, Michael Neerhof, and Chelsea Seale.

Macdonald Stewart Art Centre is supported by its sponsors: the University of Guelph, the City of Guelph, the County of Wellington, and the Upper Grand District School Board; by memberships and donations; and by grants from the Ontario Government through the Ontario Arts

Council and the Ministry of Citizenship, Culture, and Recreation; and from the Federal Government through the Canada Council for the Arts and the Department of Canadian Heritage.

Daniel Fischlin and the Canadian Adaptations of Shakespeare Project gratefully acknowledge the substantial support of the Social Sciences and Humanities Research Council of Canada, the Premier's Research Excellence Awards, the Office of the Vice-President of Research at the University of Guelph, and the College of Arts Dean's Office at the University of Guelph.

Daniel Fischlin
Director, Canadian Adaptations of Shakespeare Project
Professor and University Research Chair, School of English and
Theatre Studies
University of Guelph

Judith Nasby
Director and Curator, Macdonald Stewart Art Centre
Adjunct Professor, School of Fine Art and Music
University of Guelph

Shakespeare MADE IN CANADA

On Shakespearean Adaptation
and Being Canadian

Adaptation and the Shakespeare Effect

SHAKESPEARE IS ARGUABLY one of the great iconic artists of all time in any field, any historical moment, and any culture—a beloved "universal" figure on par with the authors of the Popol Vuh, the enigmatic scripture of post-classic Mayan civilization; with the Kemetic artists of ancient Egypt who adorned the pyramids with hieroglyphs that give eloquent testimony to the deep learning of that culture; with the Yoruba and other African rhythmatists whose sense of metrics and spirituality gave birth millennia later to jazz; and with a small elite of great Western artists like Michelangelo, da Vinci, Dante, Bach, Beethoven, James Joyce, Louis Armstrong, among others.

But to say as much is to beg all sorts of questions. What does it mean to have achieved this unique place in global culture? Who decides on this ranking and why are other artists (especially women) left off the list? What are the uses to which this cultural influence is put? What does it mean to have "universal" appeal? What makes any of this meaningful to contemporary culture, so shaped by technology, industrialization, and corporatism—all of which emerged as forms of social organization during Shakespeare's own time?

Is it fair any longer to think of Shakespeare simply as the flesh-and-blood creator of *Hamlet* or *Titus Andronicus,* when in fact his cultural influ-

LEFT Anthony Newman (age 7), *Macbeth Killing King Duncan* (2004)

3

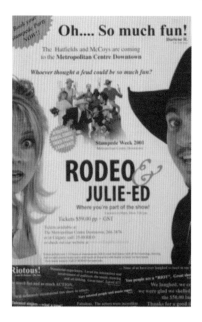 

LEFT Production poster for *Rodeo and Julie-Ed* directed by Peter Skagen (Metropolitan Centre Downtown, Calgary, 1999)

RIGHT Production poster for *Danespotting* directed by Matthew MacFadzean and Amy Price-Francis (The Infinite Space, Montreal, 1997)

ence is diffused over so many areas that he has become something other than the writer of great plays, the creator of memorable characters? This other thing that Shakespeare has become, that makes him both what he *is* and *is not,* is the "Shakespeare effect." This effect could not exist without the legacy of Shakespeare's written, published, and performed works—works that have been given a life of their own by people who engage with them in ways that Shakespeare could never have foreseen. The Shakespeare effect is everywhere evident: from the ever-increasing volume of movies that adapt his works, through to his use in commercial advertising culture, his corporate influence through the many businesses associated with his name, and his general cultural presence that makes him a signifier for literary and artistic achievement.

In Canada, this diffusion is particularly evident, with hundreds of adaptations of Shakespeare's works having been written since pre-Confederation, the creation of a major classical Shakespearean Festival in the early 1950s in Stratford, Ontario, and the interweaving of Shakespearean referents into all aspects of popular culture, from song (Rufus Wainwright) to television comedy (the Royal Canadian Air Farce) to intercultural film (Deepa Mehta). In Canada, if you don't have *Shakespeare for Breakfast,* you can have him for dinner (as in Peter Skagen's *Rodeo and Julie-Ed,* a dinner theatre adaptation of *Romeo and Juliet*); you can go

Danespotting or catch Hamlet in an unguarded moment in *Denmark and Elsinore* (Debora Grant's R&B adaptation of *Hamlet*); or you can face off with the Bard in Chris Coculuzzi's *Shakespeare's Comic Olympics* or in Ken Hudson's hockey-themed version of *Henry V*.

Shakespeare can be found as an affirmation of identity in French, Aboriginal, and Afro-Canadian cultures, as well as in a host of other multicultural and transcultural locations. The extraordinary theatrical venture *38*, a single multi-authored event coordinated by Théâtre Urbi et Orbi and Théâtre d'Aujourd'hui over five nights, featured thirty-eight authors, each under the age of thirty-eight, who were commissioned to create adaptations of Shakespeare's thirty-eight plays. Aboriginal artists, such as Yves Sioui Durand and Yvette Nolan, repurpose Shakespeare to critique colonial injustice and heal the effects of that injustice (including tribal genocide). Djanet Sears's *Harlem Duet* is a reinterpretation of *Othello*, while Azra Francis's *A Caribbean Midsummer Night's Dream* is an adaptation of *A Midsummer Night's Dream*. Allen Booth and Robin White's 1984 version of *Romeo and Juliet, Hô Mão and Julieta: A Multi-cultural Romeo and Juliet* works in a wide assortment of aesthetic and political contexts. And these are just a smattering of hundreds of such variations, adaptations, and transgressions that place Shakespeare's plays in distinctively Canadian contexts.

LEFT Production poster for *Shakespeare's Comic Olympics* directed by Chris Coculuzzi (Trinity College Playing Field, Toronto, 2004)

RIGHT Production poster for *A Caribbean Midsummer Night's Dream* directed by Azra Francis (Joseph Workman Auditorium, Toronto, 1983)

The merging of Shakespeare's legacy with creative reinterpretation is primarily the work of adaptation, a mode of literary culture-making that repurposes existent material in new ways. This adaptive form of making is one with which Shakespeare was extremely familiar, his own plays rely extensively on source works that he assiduously chose for reinterpretation. I'm often asked to define what adaptation means. The short answer is "anything you can get away with in the name of another artist's influence." This definition often prompts anxiety. How can such a loose definition be functional? Shouldn't artistic creation have firmer rules in place? Shouldn't the theory around what an adaptation is be less elastic? My response is simple: adaptation in the name of another artist's influence cannot be predicted, cannot be predetermined, cannot be constrained.

Adaptation is creative energy unleashed across a full spectrum of artistic possibility: from the most orthodox and conventional, the most slavish to the "original," through to the most extreme and anarchic undoing in the name of artistic play and freedom.

So, if Shakespeare has come to hold a unique global cultural prominence, an iconic power encoded in the works he has left us and in the works his texts have engendered as adaptive inventions, what meaning is to be got from that code today? And especially so in the context of Canadian theatrical culture, which has invested so heavily in making Shakespeare central while simultaneously working so hard to find ways to shape-shift Shakespeare into the multiple and complex contexts that make Canada what it is.

Canadian Adaptations of Shakespeare Project (CASP)

The Shakespeare—Made in Canada exhibition attempts to address these questions from a multitude of perspectives. Whether it be in the way in which contemporary theatre designers in Canada have sought to reflect Canada's changing multicultural realities in their interpretation of Shakespeare; the way in which the unique thrust stage design created by the Stratford Festival of Canada has globally influenced audiences' sense of how they interact with the actors on the stage; the way in which the amazingly varied responses to Shakespeare's work in a specific geo-cultural space (Canada) have taken his work as a place of inspiration, resistance, argument, and dialogue, and have made something anew of him; whether it is in the way virtually all students in English-speaking countries, Canada included, encounter Shakespeare as a core component of their education; or the way in which a small piece of painted wood has traversed continents and centuries all while remaining in one family's possession since the time of Shakespeare to arrive in Canada as potentially the most authentic image of the Bard—all of these show Shakespeare to be emphatically here and now in Canada, a cultural presence

The main page of the CASP website <www.canadianshakespeares.ca>.

that cannot be denied, a cultural effect that continues, for better or worse, to have influence on the way in which various civic discourses in Canada are shaped.

Not to forget that Shakespeare's cultural influence is pervasive. He is the most inventive shaper and user of the English language ever—a language that has taken on global pertinence like no other language—the language of global commerce, science, and technology, and a kind of global lingua franca. Recall Shakespeare's roots in Elizabethan popular culture: he was emphatically an artist who flowed between the "Liberties"—the ungovernable suburban spaces of London where outdoor public theatres were located—and the court, where he curried favour like few others in spite of his Catholic religious sympathies. But Shakespeare is also present at the birth of corporate culture, as we perhaps *don't* know it.

Alongside the British East India Company, whose history of imperial trade and plunder extended over the centuries following its establishment by Royal Charter in 1600, the Globe Theatre, in which Shakespeare was a shareholder, was one of the first "corporations." The Globe Theatre was founded as a joint stock venture in 1599 and played its own role in staging forms of theatrical nationalism that justified and commented (sometimes critically) on historical genealogies related to British self-interest. Shakespeare has always been implicated in national cultures: from his own obsessive interest in writing history plays, through to the global importance that his language has taken on, to the ways in which particular cultures have appropriated his works for the purpose of linking aesthetic excellence to nation.

The Canadian Adaptations of Shakespeare Project (CASP) at the University of Guelph is the first research project of its kind anywhere in the world devoted to the systematic exploration and documentation of the ways in which Shakespeare has been adapted into (and out of) a national, multicultural theatrical practice. One of the defining features of Canada's cultural heritage is the extent to which it relies on a dialogue with traditional Shakespearean theatre mutated into multiple adaptations that stage what it means to be "Canadian." For better or worse, Canada's theatrical past is profoundly connected to Shakespeare, with productions, revisions, adaptations, and any number of spin-off representations a key feature of the Canadian cultural landscape. The *Canadian Theatre Encyclopedia* entry on Shakespeare states:

> The most produced non-Canadian playwright, his works are at the foundation of theatre in this country [Canada] and are performed in all styles at virtually all the major theatres, in French and in English, across the nation. Like Molière, the works of Shakespeare appear as keystones throughout the history of theatre here [in Canada]. His were among the first works performed in the New World, they were the raison d'être of the foundation of the nation's largest theatre (Stratford Festival), and they are still being taught in schools, with interpretations which change from era to era.

As much as this Shakespearean presence is a function of Canada's colonial heritage with its dependency on immigrant cultures, it is also a function of how a new and emergent culture has sought to define itself in dialogue with—and frequently against—the Shakespearean tradition. CASP is an attempt to document the fascinating permutations this dialogue has taken with the understanding that Shakespeare is situated at a key nexus in a wide array of cultural activities and referents, called the Shakespeare effect.

Adaptation, though far from uniquely so, is a distinctively Canadian approach to theatrical production. In an article discussing adaptation in Canadian theatre, playwright Michael Healey says that "as the third wave of Canadian playwrights emerges, the desire to tell our own stories continues, but alongside that is the recognition that we can successfully bring our own sensibilities to texts that already exist."[1] This same article observes that while translation and adaptation in French Canadian theatre have been standard for years as a means of bringing international works to francophone audiences, English Canadian adaptations and translations are relatively new. In each case, however, these adaptive modes work to refigure the "original" work through the mediation of specific cultural influences and contexts.

Canadian scholarship, too, has played a crucial role in providing the necessary social, historical, economic, religious, and archival contexts for understanding the theatrical work Shakespeare produced. The Records of Early English Drama project housed at the University of Toronto, for instance, "provide proof that a man like Shakespeare—without a university education, untrained in the classical theatre tradition of the time, unacquainted with the manners of aristocracy—actually could have written the plays that are now universally regarded as the greatest in drama and literature."[2]

CASP, then, was conceived as an attempt to produce an archive of lost or forgotten theatrical materials and practices important both to Canada's theatrical and literary histories, but also to Canada's emergent sense of itself as a nation as mediated by these same materials and practices. To that end, we have collected information on close to five hundred plays in which some form of Shakespearean adaptation is at work, as well as many more cultural referents that are to be found in mass media, film, television, pop music, visual culture, and so forth. These plays and artifacts span over three centuries in chronology and document a vast range of local, regional, national, transnational, and multicultural theatrical realities that form a significant part of Canada's cultural heritage. The sheer quantity of theatrical activity occurring in the genre of Shakespearean adaptation over an extended historical period marks a significant economic, artistic, cultural, and social investment in doing "something" to/with Shakespeare.

I would note that this wide-ranging activity is over and above the theatrical work in which more conventional stagings and productions of Shakespeare occur—themselves always potential adaptations in their own right. Moreover, these adaptations, if anything, reinforce the cru-

Television and film adaptations featuring prominent Canadian Shakespeareans.

Screen stills from L to R: William Shatner in *Star Trek VI: The Undiscovered Country* (1991); Walter Pidgeon (far right) in *Forbidden Planet* (1956); two of William Shatner in *Free Enterprise* (1998); two of Paul Gross in *Slings & Arrows* (2003–2006); Colm Feore in *Slings & Arrows* (2003–2006); Christopher Plummer in *Star Trek VI: The Undiscovered Country* (1991)

cial linkage between works of the imagination and the political and social contexts out of which they emerge. Djanet Sears's *Harlem Duet,* an adaptation of Shakespeare's *Othello* in the form of a tragic, rhapsodic blues prequel, is an example of a critically aware theatre project that moved from the margins of "professional" theatre to the very centre of it at the Stratford Festival. That Sears led the first production by a Black playwright and an all-Black cast in Stratford's fifty-four-year history with an adaptation of Shakespeare is an example of Shakespeare's cultural capital in action. That *Harlem Duet* was staged in Stratford's Studio Theatre highlights the hierarchy that remains firmly in place even when new Canadian work that reflects issues of cultural identity makes it to mainstream theatre venues. Adaptations challenge orthodoxies of interpretation, but they also ask us to reconsider the material realities of where and how theatre is made and who gets to make it. The extent to which Shakespeare's capital is used to diversify, however minimally, what audiences see on Canadian main stages is worth noting as an example of the broader cultural effects associated with Shakespearean adaptation.

Both Shakespeare's use of a wide variety of source texts and adaptive techniques in his theatrical writing and the recent explosion of Shakespearean adaptation studies provide another important context for understanding the impetus behind CASP. The diversity of Shakespearean adaptation in Canada is staggering: from Aboriginal and Afro-Canadian theatre through to colonial, postcolonial, fringe, multicultural, minority, popular culture, gay, lesbian, Queer, and youth theatre. The CASP digital archive includes adaptations with a range of thematic predilections: from cowboy Shakespeare to vampire Shakespeare to club (rave and DJ) Shakespeare to hockey Shakespeare to TheatreSports Shakespeare (TheatreSports being a uniquely Canadian theatrical invention) to Shakespeare and the October

Crisis of 1970 to all-female, "chickspeare" versions of *Julius Caesar* (Vinetta Strombergs, 1986) and *A Midsummer Night's Dream* (Kate Lynch, 2001), and all-Black versions of *Hamlet* and *Othello.*

If it is Canadian musicians who have a Shakespearean connection, think of, among others: the Arrogant Worms, the Barenaked Ladies, Humphrey and the Dumptrucks, Loreena McKennit, Diane Nalini, and the Williams. Even Oscar Peterson made a seminal trio recording on the Stratford stage in 1956. If it is Canadian television with a Shakespearean predilection, think of the brilliant series *Slings & Arrows,* of Wayne and Shuster's Shakespearean sketches including the still hilarious "Shakespearean Baseball Game" first performed in 1958, or of any number of sketches by the Royal Canadian Air Farce.

If it is Canadians doing Shakespeare on film, think of work by the National Film Board of Canada, including the 1999 film *Shylock* by Pierre Lasry and the 1954 Morton Parker film *The Stratford Adventure.* Consider the McKenzie brothers' film starring Rick Moranis and Dave Thomas, *Strange Brew,* a canny comedic version of *Hamlet* with toques and stubbies. Or think of William Shatner and Christopher Plummer, both Stratfordian/Shakespearean actors who appeared in various versions of *Star Trek.* At the entrance to the Shakespeare—Made in Canada exhibition, brief clips of these examples and more are shown in a video montage created by CASP to document the amazing array of cultural production related to Shakespeare in Canada. The question remains how these varied cultural productions question and destabilize what Shakespeare is and how he circulates in Canadian pop culture.

And if it is Shakespeare in Canadian art you want, look no further than Guelph-born Rolph Scarlett's modernist set designs; Joseph Légaré's painting of what has traditionally been interpreted to be the great English Shakespearean actor Edmund Kean (given the name

Joseph Légaré, *Landscape with Orator Addressing the Indians* (formerly titled *Edmund Kean Reciting Before the Hurons*), circa 1842-1843 (oil on canvas)

Alanienouidet by the Wendat) reciting before the Hurons (Wyandot/ Wendat); Cornelius Krieghoff's painting *The Shakspeare Club, Montreal, 1847*; Lawrence Hyde's dramatic woodcuts of scenes from Shakespeare; Tony Scherman's haunting encaustic evocations inspired by *Macbeth*; John Graham's beautifully rendered artist's book *Visions from The Tempest*; or David Garneau's version of Louis Riel transformed by an off-portrait viewer into Caliban, the figure of the indigene in *The Tempest.*

In response to this diversity, of which the examples above are merely the tip of the proverbial iceberg, we have designed both our website and our contribution to the Shakespeare—Made in Canada exhibition to have multiple uses for a range of audiences—from students and teachers looking for access to classroom materials through to theatre-goers and practitioners looking for production details and other sorts of information. We have collected materials with inclusiveness as a key operating principle. Thus, no rigid definitions are used in relation to key concepts like *adaptation, Canadian,* and *Shakespearean.* Indeed, many of our archival findings challenge such rigid definitions and open the door to productive interpretive debates in relation to how these three key terms intersect. If anything, the incredible variety of adaptive shapes spun out in the name of the Shakespeare effect tell us that monolithic notions of "what" Shakespeare is or "what" it means to

be Canadian simply aren't tenable when examined through the looking glass of diverse adaptive practices in Canada.

Cornelius Krieghoff,
The Shakspeare Club, Montreal,
1847 (oil on canvas)

Visions of Shakespeare / Re-visions of Canada

CASP's research offers windows through which to view the critical and creative work of a diverse range of Canadian communities through the prism of Shakespeare. To that end, we have organized our portion of the Shakespeare—Made in Canada exhibition to include a small sampling of the kinds of artifacts we have been able to gather through our research.

As you stroll the gallery space you will encounter a number of areas with distinctive themes. The first section, "Posters, Programs, and Placemats," gives the viewer a chance to see a range of the kinds of productions we have documented. Think of the effort that went into their making: from Matthew MacFadzean's post-punk, rave aesthetic, to Ben Taylor and Michelle Smith's "hip-hopera" version of *A Midsummer Night's Dream,* to Toronto director Richard Rose's *Hysterica,* a collective work that rewrites the gender dynamics of *King Lear,* with Lear figured as a modern-day Greek matriarch and immigrant to Canada. Rose's adaptation teaches an important lesson: contemporary Canadian identity must address diversity, and Shakespeare's oeuvre is a creative locus that offers a way of seeing and experiencing identity as a narrative that we must continue to tell ourselves in order to understand who we are.

The second section in the CASP installation is devoted to Shakespeare in pre- and early Confederation Canada. Not many people know this, but Shakespeare had a presence in Canada before Canada the modern nation-state was formed. You will find a number of fascinating artifacts related to Canada's colonial past, including an early Canadian text called *Ottawah, the Last Chief of the Red Indians of Newfoundland* (1848), a romantic novel that uses the structure of Shakespeare's *The Tempest* to tell the story of the genocide of the Beothuk. The Beothuk (meaning "people") were the indigenous inhabitants of Newfoundland at the time of first contact with Europe in the fifteenth and sixteenth centuries, a civilization made extinct in 1829, some twenty years before *Ottawah* was published. That Shakespeare's *The Tempest* is made to service the retelling of this tragedy tells us that nineteenth-century Canadians understood, at least partially, how Shakespeare's work related to their own colonialist contexts.

How Canada's early identity formation was profoundly linked to Aboriginal cultures through failed moments of encounter are especially evident in the story of nineteenth-century writer and politician Nicholas Flood Davin. Davin is a key background figure to the short video *What Means This Shouting?*, co-produced by Marion Gruner and Sorouja Moll for CASP. The video documents some of the points of contact among Shakespeare, Canadian colonial culture, and Aboriginal cultures. Davin wrote an adaptation of *Romeo and Juliet,* called *The Fair Grit, or the Advantages of Coalition, A Farce,* published in 1876. The play spoofs Canadian politics and concludes that the Grits and the Tories are essentially cut from the same political cloth—a canny observation from the nineteenth century that haunts us well into the twenty-first. At the behest of Sir John A. Macdonald, Davin wrote the *Report on Industrial Schools for Indians and Half-Breeds* (1879), also referred to as the *Davin Report*, a document which formed the racist basis for the residential school system that caused and continues to produce such enormous suffering to Aboriginal communities throughout the country. The connection drawn between Davin's work as an adaptor of Shakespeare and as the author of this odious document is the same connection that links Shakespearean referents to nationalist discourses of various kinds in Canada.

The CASP installation also includes rare political cartoons by John Wilson Bengough, who used Shakespearean references to satirize late nineteenth-century political events in Canada. Take a look at these and think of our own times and how prescient some of Bengough's insights are. Ask yourself why Bengough thought Shakespeare such a useful medium for transmitting this sort of satire, especially at this point in Canada's colonial history? Was Shakespeare a kind of shared cultural icon (even then) through which this sort of subversive satire could easily reach its target audience? What compelled Canadians to implicate Shakespeare in their own work at this crucial moment in Canadian history?

Shakespeare's colonial, canonical associations are no doubt problematic and part of a long history of how Shakespeare has been deployed in Canada. Adaptors' refusal to ignore the colonial relationship that Shakespeare can invoke makes their adaptations rare potential sites of cultural and political criticism in popular discourse. In a section of the exhibition called "This Island's Mine," CASP shows some of the important places where Shakespearean adaptation occurs in various colonial, post-colonial, neo-colonial, and anti-colonial projects.

Lewis Baumander's 1987 adaptation of *The Tempest* is one example. They play was consciously set at the time of colonization off the coast of British Columbia on the Queen Charlotte Islands. Without altering Shakespeare's words, Baumander presents a New World interpretation

Sorouja Moll, *Messaging Shakespeare*, 2006 (detail)

The artist explains, "This is one panel of a triptych that presents critical research on the messaging of Shakespeare in late nineteenth-century Canadian media. The triptych explores the intertextual relationships between Nicholas Flood Davin, John A. Macdonald, and Louis Riel and questions how Shakespeare (in Canada) is sampled as imperial rhetoric enabling political agendas."

William Chesney, set model for *The Tempest* directed by Lewis Baumander (Earl Bales Park, Toronto, 1987)

of the conflict that results when a peaceful, environmentally integrated, indigenous culture confronts a threatening settler presence. Baumander shows it is possible to adapt a play without even changing its text. Designer William Chesney's set maquette for Baumander's adaptation is an evocative rendering of this encounter—note how the wrecked ship's sails form a Christian cross that dominates the forest scene. As Chesney's aesthetic interpretation shows, design decisions can produce significant shifts in meaning. This crucial form of adaptation is explored more thoroughly in the installation devoted to Canadian design in Shakespearean theatre curated by Pat Flood.

Another focus of CASP's research and on-line publication details the birthing of Canadian bourgeois culture; that is, Shakespeare's relations to theatre in early twentieth-century Canada. The artifacts in the L. W. Conolly Theatre Archives gallery document the work of Josephine Barrington and the Margaret Eaton School of Literature and Expression, and demonstrate the enculturation of elite Canadian youth using Shakespeare. Barrington was a prolific director of Shakespeare who used child actors to stage complete productions of the Bard's work in the 1930s. Tracing key figures from these productions and associations—Dora Mavor Moore being the most obvious example—this part of the exhibition captures in part the efforts to establish a professional theatre in Canada. As evidenced in the various Shakespeare Societies and Clubs that were part of this trend, much of this process used Shakespeare as a legitimizing referent on the path towards creating the Stratford Festival, the National Theatre School, the National Arts Centre, and others.

Let us not forget that the Family Compact played a key role in shaping Canadian values via the its idealization of British institutions and strong ties to the British Empire, through governmental, juridical, and cultural systems. The Family Compact was a small group of public servants and businessmen, what some have termed a "local aristocracy," who dominated the decision-making bodies of Upper Canada around 1830. Based mainly in what was then called York (Toronto), members of the Family Compact were from Canadian high society and no doubt played a major role in shaping the early theatrical and literary culture of Canada.

Reading the list of patrons and directors from the very first program published by the Stratford Festival (for its opening night version of *Richard III* starring Alec Guinness and Irene Worth), one is struck by key names from that aristocracy: Lady Eaton, wife of department store heir and president Sir John Craig Eaton; Floyd S. Chalmers, the former president of the Canadian Club, president of publishing giant Maclean-Hunter from 1952–1964, and president and founder of the Floyd S. Chalmers Foundation; Edward Johnson, the great Canadian tenor born in Guelph in 1878 and after whom a school in Guelph is still named; Hugh Labatt, Esq., the grandson of the founder of beer baron John K. Labatt (in 1950, Hugh and his brother introduced Canada to the beer, Labatt 50); Sir Ernest MacMillan; and the Right Honourable Arthur Meighen all of these names under the patronage of the Right Honourable Vincent Massey, then Governor-General of Canada. The social, class, and cultural affiliations of this sort of network and its relationship to Shakespearean culture in Canada is a fascinating aspect of Canadian theatre history to which this portion of the exhibition points.

The artifacts in the children and youth cluster of the CASP exhibition use Shakespeare in a very different way from those in the pre- and early Confederation Canada cluster. Doreen D'eath deploys the dark images and themes of *Hamlet* and *Macbeth* to engage her students in critical and creative literacy projects. Guelph resident Nick Craine's beautifully rendered chiaroscuro biography of Shakespeare, *Parchment of Light,* here given public display for the first time, aims not to elevate or support Shakespeare's revered cultural status, but rather to examine the development and formation of a creative genius who just happens to be Shakespeare. Craine's work, using the graphic novel medium so popular with youth, asks us to see beyond the texts associated with Shakespeare and to imagine what moved Shakespeare to write—or indeed, what motivates anyone to create. Arline Smith's miniature theatre, on view in the Possible Worlds installation, depicts the "Pyramus and Thisbe" scene from *A Midsummer Night's Dream,* its consummate construction as important as its adaptation of Shakespearean performance. The appeal to youth audiences is no surprise, especially given Smith's use of high-end technologies like fibre optic lighting and audio narration to convey the sense of a scene within a scene within a scene. What happens to the viewer who is seduced by the call of the miniature theatre as the scene of encounter on the Shakespearean stage replays? The coming together of creators and audience foments its own form of magic, its own technology of entrancement.

Anthony Newman (age 7),
Witch Puppet (2004)

Finally, the CASP exhibition consciously tries to show how multiple narratives associated with Shakespeare are part of the weave of Canadian culture—and it does so in the shadow of the enigmatic Sanders portrait. The collocation of the two galleries begs a number of questions. As Canadians, what benefits do we accrue from the ownership and display of the Sanders portrait? How does this mesh with our values of and relationship to Shakespeare as Canadians? We adapt, we question, and we criticize—the buzz around this image and its "authenticity" should not distract us from this critical path.

Canada's questioning of Shakespeare and of his (British) cultural authority date back to the earliest days of the Stratford Festival. The festival was founded on the celebrity of director Tyrone Guthrie and actors Alec Guinness and Irene Worth, each recognized at the time as authorities (read British) on classical theatre. The festival quickly moved away from this model with the appointment of Québécois director Jean Gascon (1920–1988) as the festival's first Canadian Artistic Director. (Let's not forget that Gascon, who had co-founded the Théâtre du Nouveau-Monde with Jean-Louis Roux, Georges Groulx, Guy Hoffmann, and Robert Gadouas in 1951, died in Stratford.) Stratford has since developed a Canadian tradition of theatre training with a method and style that is recognized around the world. While no one would argue that Stratford is home to new Canadian theatre, it no longer attempts to reproduce directly a British tradition.

Much of the Canadian discourse around the Sanders portrait's authenticity relates back to the British-owned Chandos portrait as the benchmark—more valuable discussions would be centred on what the Sanders portrait image means to Canadian culture. To whom does Shakespeare belong? How do the narratives that are such an important part of the Sanders portrait's history reflect on what it means to be Canadian in relationship to various other forms of the identity quest staged via "our" relationship to Shakespeare?

Shakespeare may, indeed, be for all time. But as the Shakespeare—Made in Canada exhibition shows, he is also very much here in Canada in the present moment, shape-shifting us perhaps as much as we shape-shift him.

Nick Craine, *The Sanders Portrait* (2006)

ENDNOTES

1 J. Kelly Nestruck, "The motto of Canada's dramatists: adapt or die," *Gazette* (Montreal), July 23, 2005.

2 Monika Stephenson. "Canadian scholarship gives the Bard a boost," *Globe and Mail,* May 1, 2004.

Daniel Fischlin is professor and research chair at the University of Guelph and founder and director of the Canadian Adaptations of Shakespeare Project. He is also co-curator of the Shakespeare—Made in Canada exhibition.

NICK CRAINE

Parchment of Light:
The Life & Death of William Shakespeare

SHAKESPEARE WORKED, in substantial part, in the gutter of the arts in his own time. His decision to work in the theatre was not a passive act of whimsy. Rather, theatre was his entry point to survival. Having no standing in the world and no interest in following in his father's footsteps, the theatre allowed him to capitalize on his most valuable asset—his wit. It also permitted him to foster a rich internal life. In exchange for this safe harbour, Will elevated the theatrical medium from disposable pop to meaningful, complex narrative and, eventually, masterpiece.

The decision to depict Will Shakespeare's life as a graphic novel, with all the rich visual and literary resonances of the genre, is the guiding aesthetic of *Parchment of Light*. To portray the Bard's life in a comic strip narrative makes the telling itself a relentless artistic action emerging from the margins of so-called high culture, as did theatre in Shakespeare's own time. Using the basic vocabulary of comics, I insert complex narrative structures and call on alternative modes of visual depiction to

Parchment of Light: The Life & Death of William Shakespeare is a graphic novel conceived, written, and illustrated by Nick Craine. *Parchment of Light* interprets and adapts the known facts of Shakespeare's life to create a revealing and personal portrait of the Bard.

LEFT Nick Craine, a page from *Parchment of Light: The Life & Death of William Shakespeare*, a graphic novel work-in-progress

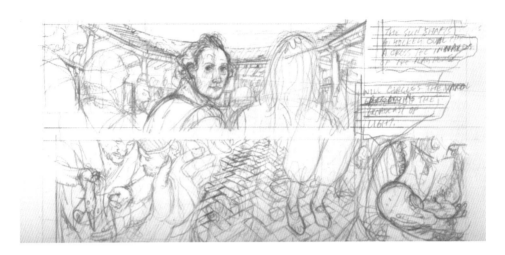

create a meaningful portrayal—in essence "drawing" high art out of bubble gum. The action in the graphic novel subverts expectations and perhaps parallels Will's own experiences as he traversed the terrain from popular to courtly culture.

Parchment of Light also attempts to gather literary capital from an association with Shakespeare in the same way in which the Bard's history plays gained capital from centering on King Henry or Titus Andronicus. Shakespeare's history plays garnered the playwright validation as a maker of high art, a distinction that he sought.

Parchment of Light consolidates the study and conjecture of Shakespearean lore into one expansive visual telling—a go-to reference text for the Elizabethan period. Not just a play-by-play of the collected facts of his life, *Parchment of Light* also views Will as a punk rocker—a grub in a world full of cultural anxiety and religious dynamism—an obsessive observer who loved human beings and, ultimately, someone who strove to become a gentleman and, in so doing, found acceptance of himself.

Craine's *Parchment of Light* is an adaptation in both content and process. Each page starts as a pencil sketch, becomes an ink drawing, and, in final rendering, is completed with the addition of hand-lettered text.

Nick Craine is an artist and musician living in Guelph, Ontario. He is the author of two acclaimed graphic novel adaptations, *Dance Me Outside: The Illustrated Screenplay* and *Portrait of a Thousand Punks: Hard Core Logo*. His illustrations have appeared in the *New York Times Review of Books*, the *Washington Post*, and *Quill & Quire*.

| LLOYD SULLIVAN

The Sanders Portrait:
This *Is* the Face of the Bard

The Importance to Canada of having
the Most Authentic Image of the Bard

> How beauteous mankind is! O brave new world,
> that has such people in't!
> *The Tempest,* Act V, scene 1

William Shakespeare shook the dust of the old world of literature from his feet and boldly created a brave new one. It is interesting, and perhaps symbolic, that the Sanders portrait was "discovered" in the "new world." It seems as if the image in the Sanders portrait represents the youthful vigour and vitality of the Americas, while the Droeshout engraving and the memorial bust, literally and allegorically, denote a certain faded colonial glory.

Coincidentally, the age of the Sanders portrait roughly matches that of Canada. In 1603 when it was painted, the great explorer Samuel de Champlain had just set his first tentative steps in New France. A small trading post or two represented the entire European presence. With a sense of faith and adventure, the settler families persevered and established a society with its foundations in the Old World but informed by the new land they inhabited.

LEFT The Sanders portrait

The portrait itself travelled across the Atlantic with just such a family of adventurous, faith-filled immigrants who were in search of a new life in a land of abundant opportunity. We do know that by the year 1786 the first professional theatre company in Canada had performed Shakespeare's plays. His plays have been performed here continuously ever since. One of the largest Shakespeare festivals in the world takes place each year in Stratford, Ontario. The University of Guelph, the initiator and sponsor of the Shakespeare—Made in Canada exhibition, hosts the largest website in the world devoted to Shakespeare in a specifically national Canadian context <www.canadianshakespeares.ca>. Shakespeare's works are studied by students and enjoyed by theatre-goers across the country.

There is a great fascination with the Sanders portrait in Canada and even pride and joy that it was discovered here. The portrait attracted large crowds when it was exhibited at the Art Gallery of Ontario in Toronto during the summer of 2001. The book, *Shakespeare's Face,* by Stephanie Nolen was a Canadian bestseller. Many people would like to see the Sanders portrait remain in Canada in order to preserve its educational and historic value as part of an unparalleled legacy bequeathed to us and our children. The portrait provides a tangible expression of the deep British roots in our collective history and the arts.

A Portrait in Authenticity

> He is mischievous, keen-eyed, almost flirtatious. Half twinkle, half smirk, he looks out from his portrait with a tolerant, world-weary air. This is Shakespeare. Perhaps you thought you knew him: bald pate, thin brows, stiff white ruff. You thought wrong.
> —*Globe and Mail,* 2001

> It's a wonderfully romantic portrait. He looks amused and amusing and intelligent, just the way we'd rather like Shakespeare to look.
> —Professor Anne Lancashire, University of Toronto

> The Sanders portrait puts a human face on English literature.
> —Professor Alexander Leggatt, University of Toronto

I was caught by the eyes. There does seem to be
something about the eyes that seems to resemble the
eyes in the two other known representations.
—Professor Morgan Holmes, Ryerson University

The Sanders portrait shows a dashing, enigmatic young
man who looks like he might have just walked off the
film set of *Shakespeare in Love.*
—Stephen Sheding

[The Sanders portrait] displays a handsome visage,
intelligent quixotic eyes and an enigmatic Mona Lisa
smile.
—Paul H. Altrocchi, M.D.

Not many would argue with the statement that William Shakespeare
is the greatest English poet and dramatist. He is widely celebrated for
the immense range of his subject matter and style; his extraordinary
ability to get inside his characters without judgment or bias; his way of
bringing together a whole range of ideas and issues without imposing
himself upon them; and his sheer creativity with language.

Renaissance dramatist, playwright, and poet Ben Jonson placed
Shakespeare above Chaucer and Spenser, and above the great Greek
and Roman dramatists. "He was not of an age, but for all time," Jonson
wrote only a few years after his friend's death, and he could not have
been more visionary in his assessment. Shakespeare's influence on
English literature and culture goes beyond that of any other single creative artist. In his own time, his plays were highly popular at the public
theatres and at court. Today, his words speak to us with the same wit,
wisdom, and insight as they did to our ancestors four hundred years
ago.

But who was the historical figure behind these timeless writings?
What does the face of genius look like? For centuries people have asked
these questions. Frustratingly, William Shakespeare has proven to be
one of the most elusive characters in history. Many details of his life
are shrouded in mystery. We have only two images of Shakespeare that
are universally accepted as authentic. They are the Martin Droeshout
copper engraving and the stone memorial bust of Shakespeare at Holy

Trinity Church at Stratford-upon-Avon. Unfortunately, both were created after his death and are considered poor in quality.

This is the story of the Sanders portrait, which the Sanders family and its Canadian descendants firmly believe to be a true-life image of the Bard of Avon. According to Sanders family tradition, the portrait was painted by an ancestor, a friend of Shakespeare and bit player in his company of actors. The portrait, the family, and their stories are intertwined; together they have survived fire, flood, and a transatlantic voyage. The Sanders have always kept their portrait close to them—sometimes proudly displayed in their homes, at other times tucked away in cupboards or under beds for safe-keeping.

Quietly, the Sanders portrait passed from generation to generation to the present owner, Lloyd Sullivan, who acquired it from his mother, Kathleen Hales Sanders. The portrait's provenance, having been passed through the centuries within a single family, is an extraordinary story—one that few portrait histories could duplicate.

In 1603, the date of the Sanders portrait, Shakespeare was thirty-nine years old. No longer "the upstart crow" who shook the London theatrical establishment a decade earlier, in 1603, he was a prominent member of it. He had achieved artistic and financial success as an actor, playwright, and partner in the Globe Theatre. His literary legacy then consisted of twenty-four plays, including *Hamlet* and *Romeo and Juliet,* and he was on the verge of penning his great tragic masterpieces. This is the Shakespeare who had just purchased the second largest house in his hometown of Stratford. He had achieved the status of gentleman through the award of a coat of arms. This is also the year that Shakespeare and his company were granted the right to use the prestigious designation "The King's Men" by the new king, James I, who reigned from 1603 to 1625.

The face in the Sanders portrait bears a striking similarity to a famous contemporary description of Shakespeare. He displays the quintessential look of an Englishman of the Midlands: fine features, fair of hair and complexion. The eyes are bluish-green with a mischievous twinkle and a surprising intensity of gaze. The head is capped by a shock of receding auburn hair. The mouth is slightly upturned in a kind of "Mona Lisa" smile. According to the *London Times,* February 5, 2006, "the face that emerges as if by candlelight from the dark shadow in this picture is utterly individual, marked with humour and sorrowful wisdom, self-confidence, intelligence and candour." Or, put more simply, another reviewer has said that the man in the Sanders portrait seems ready to "burst into words."

The costume in the Sanders portrait is a striking woven doublet with a stiff Elizabethan collar. Experts at the Globe Theatre in London have attempted to recreate the decorative pattern of the doublet using a number of different materials and methods that were available in the early 1600s. They have concluded that only silver thread on silk satin could reproduce the look of the doublet in the portrait.

Until 1604, England had strictly enforced the sumptuary laws, which at that time placed personal limitations on the wearing of colours, fabrics, and styles of decoration. Elizabethans were quick to modify their wardrobe as soon as a small change in social rank permitted new options. Silver lace on silk satin was something only a gentleman could legally wear. The date of the Sanders portrait, 1603, was the earliest that a social-climbing Shakespeare would have been permitted such ornamentation. The Globe experts have also confirmed that the hairstyle in the portrait is consistent with the date for someone of Shakespeare's rank and status.

The Sanders portrait has been subjected to a significant number of scientific tests—more than any other image associated with Shakespeare. All the tests prove that the portrait was painted around 1603, and that the artist used materials, techniques, and a style consistent with that of the Northern School of Art, which was prevalent throughout England during that time period. Radiocarbon analysis confirms that the label on the back of the portrait dates from approximately the same era as the painting itself. There is no evidence of overpainting or alteration of any kind since its date of creation.

The Sanders portrait measures 42 cm by 33 cm (16 ½" by 13") and is painted in oil on two oak panels carefully prepared with a layer of calcium carbonate and glue, followed by a layer of lead white and calcium carbonate in oil. The date "Anno 1603" appears in the upper right hand corner in reddish paint.

Portions of the edges of the oak panels are slightly worm-eaten. It also appears that approximately two inches of the panel on the right side may have been damaged or worn away.

An exhaustive genealogical investigation of the Sanders family has traced the family tree back to the late 1500s in the Worcester area, a few miles from Shakespeare's hometown of Stratford-upon-Avon. Documents confirm the existence of a Sanders or Saunders in Shakespeare's company of actors. A Sanders family story retells that the names Sanders and Shakespeare appear next to each other in a Swansea Inn visitor's book originally found in London, England. A tantalizing 1745 document describes the estate of a Sanders ancestor as including "8 pictures," though the subject or titles of the paintings are not revealed.

The portrait has been publicly exposed on only a few occasions over its long history. In 1909, the current owner's great-grandfather, Thomas Hales Sanders, lent the portrait to the noted Shakespearean expert M. H. Spielmann, who wrote an article on it for *The Connoisseur* magazine (Volume XXIII, January–April, 1909). Spielmann also mentioned the Sanders portrait in the 1911 *Encyclopedia Britannica* (eleventh edition, volume 24). It appears that the earliest public display of the portrait took place at the Stern Brothers Gallery in New York City in 1928. It was displayed again in the early 1960s at the Art Gallery in the Eaton's department store in downtown Montreal.

In 2001, the *Globe and Mail,* Canada's national newspaper, published a series of in-depth articles on the portrait. Media outlets around the world then picked up the story. In the summer of that year, the Sanders portrait was the focal point of an exhibition at the Art Gallery of Ontario in Toronto, attracting a large number of visitors, including many Shakespeare scholars and art enthusiasts.

During the following year, the Stratford Festival of Canada chose the Sanders portrait to illustrate the promotional posters and souvenirs for its fiftieth anniversary season. Also in 2002, the book *Shakespeare's Face* was published. In it, author Stephanie Nolen recounts the legend and history of the Sanders portrait. The book was a bestseller in Canada and was subsequently translated into a number of different languages and published throughout the world.

In early 2006, the Sanders portrait was featured as part of the greatly anticipated Searching for Shakespeare exhibition, organized by the National Portrait Gallery in London, England. This exhibition included a host of important Shakespeare and theatre artifacts. It also assembled, for the first time in one location, the elite group of reputed life portraits of Shakespeare: the Chandos, the Flower, the Soest, the Grafton, the Jansen, and the Sanders. In June 2006, the exhibition travelled to the Yale Center for British Art in New Haven, Connecticut, prior to its arrival in Guelph for the Shakespeare—Made in Canada exhibition.

The Sanders portrait, painted in 1603, depicts the Bard in the prime of his life both physically and creatively. Some of the great tragedies, like *Othello* and *Macbeth*, and his late plays often called the Romances (*Cymbeline, The Winter's Tale,* and *The Tempest*) were still to be written. The Sanders portrait offers far more insight into the man behind the words than the bald, bloated image that stared blankly at us from the cover of our high school texts. Take a look into those mischievous, intelligent eyes and you too will be convinced that this is the face of genius!

Ancestry

There is a lack of pertinent family documents concerning the Sanders portrait from the time it was mentioned in the 1915 will of the great-grandfather of the present owner, Lloyd Sullivan, back to the date of the portrait, 1603. According to oral provenance, many Sanders family documents relevant to the portrait were lost to fire and flood in the 1800s.

However, a team of investigators, including a genealogist in Worcester, has researched the Sanders portrait for the past fifteen years and has uncovered a number of interesting facts relevant to the Sanders family tree.

Kathleen Sullivan, née Hales Sanders (1903–1972)

Kathleen, mother of the current owner of the Sanders portrait, was the youngest daughter of Aloysius and Agnes Hales Sanders. She was born in Montreal on May 30, 1903, and was a multi-talented person much like her father. She was educated at St. Marguerite Bourgeoys School for girls in Montreal where she excelled in French, music, and the arts. She possessed the traditional Sanders talent for painting, which she started while attending school but did not resume again until much later in life.

In 1928, Kathleen married Alexander Sullivan in Montreal. Their only child, Lloyd Sullivan, was born on April 12, 1933. Kathleen was a gentle, peaceful, energetic woman much loved by her siblings. She was a kind person who went out of her way to help people, especially her sisters and

Kathleen Sullivan, circa 1928

31

brothers. When her mother fell ill in 1940, Kathleen became her primary caregiver until Agnes's death on March 24, 1943.

During the time that Agnes lived with her daughter's family, the Sanders portrait and other objects of family value lay hidden under her bed. Lloyd Sullivan can remember, when he was about nine or ten years old, bringing his grandmother tea, and for this act of kindness she allowed him to have a peek at the Sanders portrait. These were solemn moments for him, full of mystery and wonderment, and he was totally fascinated by it all. Little did he know that this fascination would remain with him for the rest of his life.

The Sullivan's home in Montreal was always open to Kathleen's sisters and brothers. They gathered there most weekends especially on birthdays and holidays. Family business was discussed and often centred on the portrait. A great deal of time was spent discussing what to do with the Sanders portrait. Now and then, when the rhetoric became too heated and tempers flared, Kathleen would step in and settle the matter; everything would return to normal, yet no decisions concerning the portrait were made.

Finally, a number of years after Agnes's death, the Sanders family members consented to allow Kathleen's eldest brother, Frederick, to arrange to have the Sanders portrait displayed at the Eaton's department store in downtown Montreal. Eaton's had a large picture gallery on the sixth floor and the Sanders portrait was displayed for a few weeks in the summer of 1964. During that period, Frederick was approached by a Montreal art dealer who wanted to purchase the portrait for $100,000. Frederick was anxious to sell the painting, and the Sanders family considered its proposed sale. Heated and drawn out discussions ensued, but in the end a vote was taken—the family decided not to sell the portrait.

Frederick was furious, but family members convinced him that the portrait was probably worth far more than $100,000 if it could be authenticated. In the ensuing years, the Sanders family members came to the realization, after a number of enquiries were made, that the authentification of the portrait would be an extremely costly and time-consuming endeavour.

Over the years, family interest in the portrait waned. Frederick died on June 11, 1971, and the portrait was passed to his sister, Kathleen.

Shortly before her death a year later, Kathleen said that the family wished her son, Lloyd Sullivan, to have the Sanders portrait as they believed that he would invest in its authentication.

Aloysius Hales Sanders (1864–1919)

Kathleen's father, Aloysius Hales Sanders was born on May 7, 1864, in Lowestoft, Suffolk, England. He was the only son of Thomas Hales Sanders who, among twelve other children, survived to adulthood. Aloysius was a wise and talented person. He attended Ushaw College in the north of England, which was a training centre for Catholic priests. At the completion of his MA, Aloysius decided instead to embark on a banking career. He joined the National Provincial Bank of England, the same London bank that his father had worked for many years before.

Aloysius Hales Sanders, n.d.

Aloysius married Agnes Biggs on April 11, 1884, at a Catholic church in Croydon, England. He and his wife had five children when they decided to emigrate from London to Canada in 1894. They settled in Montreal, where Aloysius started his teaching career.

Aloysius and Agnes had eight more children, a total of thirteen, although three born in England had died in infancy. Aloysius taught art, history, English, and music. In Montreal, he taught at Sarsfield School and was one of the founders of Blinkbonnie Academy and Catholic High School. He also taught at St. Kevin's School in Outremont, Montreal. Aloysius was a skilled artist and he perfected his talent by painting outdoor scenes in and around Montreal.

In 1909, Aloysius brought more than three hundred of his father's paintings from England to Montreal, and he and the Honourable Judge Curran set about selling these art works at public auction, including Aloysius' own paintings, in order to raise funds to help with financing the schools with which Aloysius was associated. Aloysius was a successful and efficient principal and was recognized as one of the top educators in Canada. In 1907, the federal government chose him to head up a new bilingual training school in Ottawa. Aloysius turned down this prestigious appointment, preferring not to uproot his wife and children who were settled comfortably in Montreal.

Aloysius inherited the Sanders portrait from his father, Thomas Hales Sanders, on his death in 1915. The following is an excerpt from his will, which is registered with the Principle Registry of the Probate Divorce and Admiralty Division of the High Court of Justice in London, England, probated on December 14, 1915:

> I give to my son Aloysius Joseph James Hales Sanders my reputed portrait of Shakespeare dated 1603. Also my large Family Bible containing a Register of births and deaths of my family, also the life size portraits of my father and mother.

The will and estate were held up in the British probate court for over four years. Family conjecture at the time was that the British government was reluctant to let the Sanders portrait leave England because of its heritage significance. However, after much protest from the family, permission for the portrait to leave England was given in late 1919, though, sadly, not soon enough for Aloysius who died earlier on March 11, 1919, in Montreal. The portrait was left to his wife, Agnes, who went to England to retrieve it later that year.

Nine years later, her eldest daughter, Mary Agnes, arranged for the portrait to be publicly exhibited, for the first time, in a theatre exhibition at Stern Brothers in New York City. The following excerpt is from an article that appeared in the *New York Times*, October 19, 1928:

> Miss Sanders, who was at Stern's yesterday for the exhibit, said that Shakespeare and Sanders were supposed to have been close friends and that their names are to be seen together in an old visitors' book at Swansea Inn, London. Shakespeare's name is on the back of the painting, on which is also written "This likeness taken 1603— Age at that time 39 y^s" She said that during her grandfather's lifetime he had been approached many times by Shakespearean societies and individuals who wished to purchase the Sanders portrait, but he always refused to part with it, as he considered it his most treasured pos-

session and did not want it to leave the family to which it had always belonged.

A year later, on January 16, 1929, Agnes gave the Sanders portrait to her daughter Mary Agnes as a gift. Fourteen years later on March 24, 1943, Agnes passed away. Mary Agnes never married and when she died in Montreal on October 19, 1959, the Sanders portrait passed to her eldest brother, Frederick. After Frederick's death in 1971, the portrait passed on to Kathleen Sullivan, mother of the present owner.

Thomas Hales Sanders (1830–1915)

Thomas Hales Sanders, the great-grandfather of the present owner, was born in Worcester on June 3, 1830, to Thomas Sanders and Mary Griffiths. Thomas joined the National Provincial Bank of England in Worcester on September 1, 1842, at the early age of twelve. In 1858, at the age of twenty-eight, he married Henrietta Martha Fitzgerald and they settled in Martley, Worcester. Their first child, Mary Agnes, was born on April 17, 1860.

Thomas Hales Sanders, circa 1913

With a young family to support, Thomas requested a better position at the bank. He was promoted to bank manager and sent to Lowestoft, Suffolk, where he stayed for over eight years until he was transferred to the bank's head office at 15 Bishopsgate, London, in 1869. Thomas retired on June 30, 1898, after fifty-one years of service.

Thomas and Henrietta had nine children, four boys and five girls. Only one boy, Aloysius Hales Sanders, and three of the girls lived to adulthood. For generations, Sanders family members have possessed talent for art, music, and teaching. Thomas loved to paint, which he did in his spare time on weekends and holidays. He was primarily a marine painter but he also made many portraits of his children. He produced beautiful watercolours and oils and exhibited at institutions such as the British Institute and the Royal Academy of Arts in London, as his father, Thomas Sanders, had previously done on several occasions. In 1908, Thomas brought the Sanders portrait to M. H. Spielmann, a London expert on Shakespeare iconography, to have it examined.

Evidence

Shakespeare's Signature

As a young teenager in Montreal, Lloyd Sullivan, the current owner of the Sanders portrait, recalls a disagreement that arose among his mother's siblings about the spelling of Shakespeare's name—spelled "Shakspere"—on the linen label attached to the back of the portrait. Before his grandmother died in 1943, she said that the spelling on the label was exactly the way William Shakespeare signed his name, as reflected in the early records of Stratford-upon-Avon. This story was passed down through the Sanders family over the years, and it was one of the reasons why her father-in-law, Thomas Hales Sanders (the owner's great-grandfather), believed the portrait to be authentic.

Some of the Sanders family members thought that perhaps the ancestor who painted the portrait in 1603 had misspelled Shakespeare's name. In 1964, they sought professional advice to resolve the matter, and were reassured that "Shakspere" was indeed the way William Shakespeare spelled his name in the early days in Stratford.

The spelling "Shakspere" also recurs with a more than common degree of consistency in the registry of the Stratford Parish Church; the entry for the poet's burial in 1616 reads: "Will Shakspere gent." "Shakspere" is the spelling on both the first and second pages of the Bard's will. The same spelling can be found in conveyancing and mortgaging documents at Stratford-upon-Avon. As such, the inscription on the Sanders portrait—"Shakspere"—is consistent with a wide range of documentation from Shakespeare's own time.

Hairstyle and Costume

Costume and hairstyle analysis have contributed to the authentication of the Sanders portrait based on what is known about fashionable dress of the period. The analysis includes information about the laws governing dress code during Shakespeare's time, including the "proclamation against excess in Apparell, 6 July 1597" made by Queen Elizabeth I.

Jenny Tiramani, director of theatre design at Shakespeare's Globe Theatre in London, England, analyzed the hairstyle and the clothing of the sitter in the Sanders portrait. After exhaustive study and research, a team of experts led by Tiramani confirmed that the sitter's hairstyle, large collar (determined to be an earlier version of the Droeshout collar), and doublet with silver thread ornamentation on it are consistent with the 1603 date on the Sanders portrait for someone of Shakespeare's rank and status.

In November 2002, Tiramani was invited to present her findings at the Picturing Shakespeare symposium held by the University of Toronto. The subject of the conference was the Sanders portrait. Many Shakespeare scholars from around the world were in attendance. Tiramani showed a number of slides depicting examples of the hairstyle and clothing worn by courtiers and gentlemen in Shakespeare's era; the examples were consistent with the hairstyle and clothing of the sitter in the Sanders portrait.

During her presentation, Tiramani displayed pieces of clothing and costumes that she had brought over from England to substantiate her claim that the clothing worn by the Sanders portrait sitter was consistent with the fashion in 1603. In fact, many surviving portraits from the time show us that men of all ages, in accordance with Elizabethan dress laws, wore the same hairstyle and type of clothing as the sitter in the Sanders portrait. The sumptuary laws, which governed what an individual was allowed to wear according to class and status, were still in place at the time of the Sanders portrait, but had been repealed by James I one year later in 1604.

Tiramani's research included a comparison of the undecorated collar worn by the Sanders sitter with early seventeenth-century theatre portraits. These portraits included three images of Shakespeare, namely the Droeshout engraving, the Chandos portrait, and the Janssen memorial bust. Portrait depictions of the playwright Ben Jonson and the actor Richard Burbage were also comparison studies. Tiramani's findings reveal that only the Droeshout collar is as fine in quality as the Sanders collar, although Droeshout's is of a later fashion. This finding is consistent with the 1623 date of the Droeshout engraving (made seven years after Shakespeare's death and twenty years after the Sanders portrait was painted). Indeed, Shakespeare was thirty-nine years old in 1603, and according to Tiramani's research, the sitter's clothing and physical features in the Sanders portrait are consistent with that historical moment, further evidencing the portrait's authenticity as an image of Shakespeare.

Tiramani's fourteen-page analysis of the Sanders portrait was published in *The Journal of the Costume Society* of London, England (2005, Number 39).

Spielmann's Erroneous Examination of the Sanders Portrait

In 1908, Thomas Hales Sanders, great-grandfather of the present owner of the Sanders portrait, brought the painting to M. H. Spielmann, a London expert on Shakespeare iconography. Spielmann conducted his analysis and wrote a lengthy commentary on his findings in a 1909 article published in *The Connoisseur,* an illustrated magazine for art collectors.

Spielmann's findings are summarized as follows:

· The sitter's costume in the Sanders portrait was painted at a later time by someone else.
· The date shown in the upper right-hand corner of the painting was a relatively modern addition.
· Spielmann considered the portrait to be only 250 years old.
· The sitter's head is apparently not painted in oil.
· The label on the back of the portrait was a recent addition and was only sixty years old when Spielmann examined the painting in 1908.
· Spielmann thought the painting was not the face of Shakespeare. The shape of the skull, the construction of the jaw and chin, and the shape of the mouth are among the irreconcilable elements that prevented Spielmann from accepting the attribution.
· The sitter in the portrait looks too young to be Shakespeare at thirty-nine years old in 1603.

At the time that Spielmann conducted his examination of the portrait, he was considered to be one of the few reliable scholars to have specialized in the portraiture of Shakespeare. His 1911 *Encyclopedia Britannica* (eleventh edition) article on the portraits of Shakespeare (in which there is a reference to the Sanders portrait) was the most exhaustive survey of its kind at the time.

Recent Scientific Examination of the Sanders Portrait

Background

In the early 1990s, the Canadian Conservation Institute (cci) conducted twelve scientific tests on the Sanders portrait. The results proved positive and consistent with the Sanders family history of the portrait, and clearly and conclusively disproved Spielmann's observations.

According to the CCI:

> The results of the tests that were done were conclusive:
> the painting was executed on wood that dated from
> the correct period; the materials and the way in which
> they were used were consistent with a painting done in
> England in the early 17th century; no anachronistic ma-
> terial was found; and the label identifying the subject of
> the portrait was made of rag paper dating from 1640 at
> the latest. All these elements indicated that the painting
> was indeed an old painting and not a relatively modern
> copy or fake.

The first experiment that the CCI conducted was to the wood panel
that the portrait is painted on. Tree-ring dating was done by Dr. Peter
Klein of the University of Hamburg, Germany, who is a leading world
expert in the field of dendrochronology. His analysis showed that the
panels were made from oak wood from the Baltic region, that the earliest possible date for the execution of the painting was 1597, and that a
date of execution in 1603 was plausible.

The only statement made by Spielmann that cannot be disproven by
scientific analysis is his comment that the sitter in the Sanders portrait
looks too young to be Shakespeare at thirty-nine years old. Scientific
testing cannot verify this, since it is a purely subjective, impressionistic,
and refutable assessment.

Shakespeare biographer, Samuel Schoenbaum (1927–1996), said
that he could not accept Spielmann's conclusions about portraits that
he had examined, since there was no scientific equipment available
to Spielmann at that time. Consequently, Spielmann's conclusions are
considered conjectural and not the product of careful scientific examination and analysis.

The Linen Label

Before the label itself was analyzed, the CCI conducted tests on the adhesive used to affix the label to the back of the portrait. Using a scalpel
to extract tiny fragments from the edge of the label, the CCI collected a
sufficient sample of the original adhesive for examination under a mi-
croscope and analyzation by infrared spectroscopy. Through this process,

a substance absorbs infrared radiation, the bonds between its atoms vibrate with a characteristic frequency, and a characteristic spectrum is produced. The spectrum the CCI observed indicated that the glue was made from a plant starch, such as rice or potatoes, a finding consistent with the manufacture of adhesives in the year 1603.

Another significant scientific test done on the Sanders portrait involved the carbon dating of the label. CCI analysis showed that the label was made from rag paper comprising linen fibres, as opposed to pulp paper of modern manufacture. Then, the label itself was dated. Dr. Roelf Beukens of the Isotrace Radiocarbon Laboratory affiliated with the University of Toronto concluded that the paper was dated no later than 1640. Consequently, the dating of the paper glued to the back of the portrait, which identifies Shakespeare as the subject of the painting, indicates that the label was probably applied to the portrait between the time it was painted in 1603 and about forty years later (in 1640, the latest possible date of its manufacture).

Although the label on the back of the Sanders portrait has deteriorated considerably, it was legible in 1909, the date of Spielmann's examination of it for his article on the portraits of Shakespeare. In his article, Spielmann identified Shakespeare as the subject of the painting, and gave the dates of his birth and death. The following is the wording of the label as recorded by Spielmann:

Shakspere
Born April 23 = 1564
Died April 23 – 1616
Aged 52
This Likeness taken 1603
Age at that time 39 y^s

Author Gary Taylor explains in his book *Reinventing Shakespeare* his reluctance to adopt the accepted spelling "Shakespeare," as opposed to what he refers to as the more authentic "Shakspere," the spelling that appears on Shakespeare's baptismal record, in his will, and on the first of two drafts of a coat of arms granted to "Shakspere." Shakespeare's family name, like many names of that period, was spelled in several ways. The spelling "Shakspere" is how it appears in most Stratford records.

In relation to the Sanders portrait, the significance of the spelling "Shakspere" constitutes one more piece of evidence pointing to the authenticity of the portrait. It indicates that the label was affixed to the Sanders portrait by someone who knew the Bard well enough to know how he spelled his name. The painter would have been a likely person, on the basis of his association with Shakespeare.

In 1999, the owner of the Sanders portrait learned that the scientific testing of the ink on the linen label affixed to the back of the Sanders portrait was problematic. The technique and scientific equipment used at the time required a large sample of the label and, even then, was not guaranteed to produce an accurate result. The owner did not want to chance destroying the fragile label as it is a major part of the provenance of the portrait, so he decided not to have the ink retested, electing to wait until the scientific technique and equipment were improved to the point where only a small sample of the label would be required to produce reliable results.

Recently, a company specializing in forensic ink analysis through transmission electron microscopy testing on small ink samples has been located. Negotiations have been conducted with this company to carry out the carbon dating of the ink on the label of the Sanders portrait; tests are ongoing as this publication goes to press.

If the ink on the linen label on the back of the Sanders portrait is dated to four hundred years, the label will be the only contemporary document of historical significance in the world that records Shakespeare's date of birth. To date, the only comparable document is Shakespeare's baptismal record held in the Stratford Parish Church registry: "baptized 26th of April, 1564 in Stratford-upon-Avon." In those days, it was customary that a child was baptized at three-days-old because of the high rate of infant deaths.

Conclusion

Jenny Tiramani, the director of theatre design at Shakespeare's Globe Theatre, with a team of experts, has confirmed that the sitter's hair style, large collar, and doublet with silver thread ornamentation on it, as depicted in the Sanders portrait, are consistent with the 1603 date for someone of Shakespeare's rank and status.

The twelve scientific tests that were conducted by the Canadian Conservation Institute on the Sanders portrait in the 1990s prove that the portrait's oak panels, the paint, the date 1603 in the upper right-hand corner of the portrait, the technique and artistic style of painting, the linen label on the back of the portrait, and the glue on the label, are all four hundred years old, consistent with the period, and are not recent additions. If the only remaining test—that of the ink on the label—proves conclusively that the ink is four hundred years old, then the authenticity of the portrait is further substantiated.

The artist who painted the Sanders portrait must have known Shakespeare intimately in order to document the authentic spelling of "Shakspere," and to identify correctly the date of his birth (April 23, 1564), the date of his death (April 23, 1616), and his age of thirty-nine years in 1603. This is a further indication that the sitter in the portrait is Shakespeare. Shakespeare's birth and death dates were unknown to historians and the public until they were first published in 1773, some one hundred and seventy years after the Sanders portrait was painted. Therefore, the dating and spelling details further indicate that the sitter in the portrait is Shakespeare; how else could the person who created the portrait know these specific intimate details about the Bard unless he had close contact with Shakespeare himself?

No other Shakespeare portrait has been subjected to the level of scientific, genealogical, and stylistic scrutiny that the Sanders portrait has. The Sanders portrait, the quiet contender, has maintained its credibility throughout a significant barrage of tests, and emerges today as the only authentic lifetime image of William Shakespeare.

Lloyd Sullivan is the Canadian owner of the Sanders portrait. This essay marks the first time that an overview of his research on the portrait's authenticity has been published.

Tongues in Trees:
A Sound Installation

TO BE HONEST, a project involving a sound installation and Shakespeare initially appealed to me mainly on an aesthetic level. I thought it would be cool to hear Shakespeare's oh-so-famous words outdoors among the trees in the sculpture park at the Macdonald Stewart Art Centre, a favourite place of mine, a place with the perfect blend of artistic expression: one created by human endeavour, the other by nature.

The idea of interventionist art, or art in unexpected places, fascinated me. I imagined someone cutting through the park, late for class, suddenly assaulted by a *What, Ho!* shouted from the trees, or romanced by a *But, soft what light through yonder window breaks...* whispered from the bushes. Once I delved into the project, I realized how actors' itinerant voices could transform the park into a stage.

THE SETTING IN Shakespeare's plays is more than mere instruction to set design—it signifies a way of life, a way of thinking, and of being. Shakespeare debates the merits of the "painted pomp" within the palace walls against the freer countryside, a place where anything can happen, life is raw, and "tongues [are] in trees" (*As You Like It*).

Created by Dawn Matheson for the Macdonald Stewart Art Centre's sculpture park, *Tongues in Trees* is a motion-triggered, audio intervention featuring Shakespeare's best known monologues recited by adult literacy learners from Action Read (Guelph).

LEFT Richard Dankert
"Romeo, Romeo, wherefore art
thou Romeo..."
Romeo and Juliet
(Act II, scene 2)

RIGHT Cheryl Turner
"I know a bank where the wild
thyme blows..."
A Midsummer Night's Dream
(Act II, scene 2)

The milieus represented on Shakespeare's stage mirror the class distinctions in his Elizabethan audience, a time when *everyone* went to the theatre. "Groundlings," or commoners, were packed in at ground level; royalty in the balconies above. Shakespeare's words were intended for all classes, a beautiful inclusiveness. You didn't have to be cultured, educated, or even know how to read to *get* Shakespeare. (The majority of his audience was "illiterate.") You just had to have the experience of being alive, to have ever pondered your purpose, or to have asked the question: "What is this quintessence of dust?" Shakespeare structured his poetic phrasing to imitate the rhythm of a human heartbeat. In my mind, this is his greatest genius: his ability to understand and articulate emotion.

What has changed is Shakespeare's audience. Today, the Bard is associated with the learned, the cultured, and the upper class. His words are quoted in the classroom, not on a downtown park bench or in the line-up at the food bank, at least not knowingly. In the theatre, the main floor seats are now the most expensive in the house. And in contemporary society, Shakespeare is used as an icon of literary achievement, and not seen as an artist of and for Everyman, Everywoman.

The Stratford Festival of Canada really is a magnificent place for lovers of Shakespeare: at peak season over one thousand employees live and breathe the Bard's words, devoted to the continuance of his art. I worked behind-the-scenes there, documenting the creative process of staging Shakespeare's play *Coriolanus.* At the gala opening of the 2006 season, the Ontario Coalition for Poverty staged a protest as a political platform before the who's who of the affluent and powerful. Police officers in riot gear erected hundreds of metres of fencing to quell the

small gathering of activists. Never had I seen such disparity: ticket-holders in gowns and tuxes, wine in hand, and resolute protesters wearing placards and banging drums. In Shakespeare's day, the debate would have been played out inside. In fact, the issue of class inequality is hotly debated in *Coriolanus,* the very production presented at the gala opening. Oh, the timeliness of Shakespeare!

LEFT Kathryn Ssedoga
"The quality of mercy..."
The Merchant of Venice
(Act IV, scene 1)

RIGHT Dave Harnden
"Tomorrow, and tomorrow, and tomorrow..."
Macbeth (Act V, scene 5)

STILL, SHAKESPEARE'S INFLUENCE has been immense, his work touching virtually everyone, begging the question: *Who owns Shakespeare?* With thousands of adaptations of his work, the answer is suggested: *Anyone who stakes claim does.* That is why I love this great debate over authenticity of authorship: *How could the son of a glove maker, a lowly player with no university education, write the greatest works of the English language?*

Tongues in Trees is set out of doors and performed by adult literacy learners from Action Read (Guelph). The eight participants (actors) share similar circumstances that contribute to their literacy challenges as adults, through learning disabilities and/or limited access to education due to troubled or low-income histories. All had heard of Shakespeare, but only two participants had some familiarity with his work: one from a family of academics, the other through *Star Trek.*

We didn't get to learn about Shakespeare in Special Ed, I was told.

I thought Shakespeare had nothing to do with my life. I figured he just wrote about history.

My girlfriend said I wasn't cultured enough for Shakespeare.

Then finally, *Cool. If I can do Shakespeare, I can do anything.*

With the help of David Prosser, director of literary services at Stratford, I selected fifteen of Shakespeare's most recognizable speeches, boiled

LEFT Shawn Turner
"To be or not to be..."
Hamlet (Act III, scene 1)

RIGHT Deborah Murray
"All the world's a stage..."
As You Like It (Act II, scene 7)

them down to their basic modes of expression, and presented them to a group of curious learners at Action Read. (The staff at Action Read was initially hesitant about the project—unsure of the level of interest and potential lack of relevance of Shakespeare's writing to their learners, they were pleasantly surprised by the attendance.) We started with Shakespeare's most quoted speech, "To be or not to be," in which Hamlet asks himself: *Should I commit suicide or not?* I asked if anyone could relate. Nearly every hand in the room was raised. From there, we discussed each speech and together threw out adjectives that described the state of mind of the speaker. Then the personal stories came, the connections made.

One Hamlet had suffered more "slings and arrows of outrageous fortune" than anyone I've ever met, his physical appearance evidence of "the thousand natural shocks that flesh is heir to." Another participant embraced Portia's plea for mercy as a post-mortem appeal at a rape trial last fall where she, the victim, was brutalized on the stand, her history of mental illness used against her.

Yet another embodied King Henry V, his whole life an uphill battle. His only weapons are dogged determination and a rag-tag army (the few people in his life that have always been at his side). He heads to court in a few weeks for an assault charge: "Once more unto the breach, dear friends, once more" to "imitate the action of the tiger; / Stiffen the sinews, summon up the blood, / Disguise fair nature with hard-favour'd rage." This is his everyday survival tactic.

Another participant chose Romeo, having loved a girl in his late teens whose disability his parents could not overlook: "star-crossed

lovers" in a 1980s special ed class at John F. Ross high school. Macbeth's despairing speech, "Tomorrow, and tomorrow, and tomorrow / Creeps in this petty pace from day to day…" seemingly written for one participant who lost everything: wife, two young children, job, self-esteem, and, finally, his sanity. "Out, brief candle!"

With each exploration of Shakespeare's monologues, they responded: "been there" and "got through that."

And so, this project that began as merely a "cool" audio installation has become the catalyst for a deeper understanding and appreciation of Shakespeare's writing in the context of community, literacy, and how we all make meaning together. Never have his plays had more relevance.

LEFT Kendra Dewar "But soft, what light through yonder window breaks…" *Romeo and Juliet* (Act II, scene 2)

RIGHT Andrew Saunders "Once more unto the breach, dear friends…" *Henry V* (Act III, scene 1)

THANKS TO Mira Clarke, Sarah Dermer, and Kimm Khagram from Action Read; Gord Rand for his acting expertise; and Daniel Fischlin, Darina Griffin, Judith Nasby, and Dawn Owen for their encouragement with the project. And especially thanks to the *Tongues in Trees* performers, my Shakespearean experts, my greatest teachers of the Bard's work to date. The technical direction for this piece was done by Nick Storring, a Toronto-based composer and improviser <www.nickstorring.com>.

Dawn Matheson is a multimedia artist and writer living in Guelph, Ontario.

PAT MORDEN

A Good Block

IN ACT IV, SCENE 6 of *King Lear,* the mad Lear utters an obscure line: "This [is] a good block." Richard Monette remembers directing William Hutt in the role in 1996. When Hutt came to the line in rehearsal, he stamped his foot on the stage, rather than touching his head as many actors do. For Monette, the gesture was right for Lear and also captured an essential truth about the Festival's unique thrust stage. "It worked," says Monette. "It was a brilliant theatrical moment."

For actors, the thrust stage that Hutt honoured with his gesture is both enormously demanding and intensely exciting. "What we consider good acting at Stratford is different from many other companies," says Antoni Cimolino. Festival actor turned general director. "Acting here has been driven by the architecture. You don't have to hurl what you are doing across the void to the audience, so everything seems more natural and easy."

With minimal sets, the actors and the story they are telling become the centre of the audience experience. Seen by audience members in three dimensions whenever they are on stage, actors must perform with extraordinary concentration and skill. "An actor cannot lie on that stage," says Hutt, the great Canadian classical actor who appeared in the first season and in most of the intervening seasons until present day.

LEFT The thrust stage in 1997

"On a proscenium stage, he has the protection of scenery at his back. Here, if he is to be successful, he must be able to respond intuitively to the size and shape of the space which surrounds him." The late Mervyn Blake, who played forty-two seasons with the Festival, agreed. "It's a frightening but very exciting stage," he wrote. "I'd be terribly nervous because I felt I couldn't move without being noticed. But the best thing to do, unless you're in the middle of a scene, is to stand still and involve yourself in the scene."

The stage gives actors the opportunity to connect with their audience with a depth and intensity not possible on a proscenium stage. Artistic Director Richard Monette remembers Paul Gross, an actor more familiar with the demands of television, adjusting to the stage while rehearsing for *Hamlet.* "For the first two weeks of rehearsal he kept asking, 'Where's the camera?,' but eventually he realized that the camera is all around. He came to love working on the stage. Once you've got the knack of it, it is a great friend not only to the verse, but also to the actor."

The interaction among actors is different too. On a proscenium stage, they play to the audience and only pretend to play to one another. On the thrust, as Michael Langham put it, "their bond of relationship is direct, true, and complete, and serves to pull the audience deeply into the experience of the play."

For many fine actors, acting on the thrust stage represents the highest level of artistic expression. "There is nothing quite like standing at the centre of that stage with Shakespeare's words and nothing else," says Colm Feore, a Stratford star who has gone on to international renown in films and on Broadway. "It is an enormously dangerous place to be, and it requires enormous technical facility. But once you digest all that, the acting can be simpler, more real, and more revealing. It is three-dimensional acting, and you take the memory of that experience to everything else you do."

Blake, Feore, Gross, and Hutt are just a few of the great actors who have delivered electrifying performances on the Festival stage. Among others: Alan Bates, Brian Bedford, Zoe Caldwell, John Colicos, Bruno Gerussi, Lorne Greene, Martha Henry, William Needles, Stephen Ouimette, Christopher Plummer, Douglas Rain, Paul Scofield, William Shatner, Maggie Smith, and Christopher Walken. Many Stratford actors have become skilled teachers, sharing the expertise they developed in the demanding Stratford environment; Nicholas Pennell, for example, taught at the universities of Michigan, Eastern Michigan and Northern Michigan, Northwestern University, McMaster University, and the University of Windsor.

"Meritorious fair design" (*The Rape of Lucrece*)

FOR DIRECTORS, TOO, the challenges of the thrust stage are significant. Arranging actors on a stage with no vanishing point or pictorial perspective can be difficult, requiring directors to think in terms of diagonal movement, rather than what Monette calls the "windshield wiper" movement of the proscenium stage. Michael Langham, who assumed the role of artistic director in 1956, later admitted that he found the stage difficult to work with. "I fought it for years," he said. "I resisted it. It took me quite a few years before I began to realize that I had to accept it and go with it and sort of marry it." John Hirsch, who took over as artistic director in 1981, was reported to have said that the only directors to whom a thrust stage was "natural" were those with "a choreographic sense, twenty years of repertory experience, and nine *Shrews* and five *Hamlets* behind them." Yet as Langham discovered, once the stage is embraced, it becomes a dynamic and exciting space with great flexibility and intimacy.

Design is also challenging on the Festival stage. On a proscenium stage, much of the atmosphere and sense of spectacle is created through elaborate sets. On a thrust stage, sets must be relatively simple, although as the scale models in this exhibition demonstrate, they can be remarkably creative and evocative. The nature of the stage makes costumes and props enormously important. Because the audience is so close, everything must be "real." Costumes must stand up to scrutiny from inches away, but also to the exigencies of an eight-month season. Rich fabrics, wonderful colours, and exquisite detailing help create the imaginary world of each play. The Festival has a corps of highly skilled artisans—experts in wig making, millinery, shoemaking and leatherwork, bijoux (jewellery and gems), cutting and sewing, and costume decorating and painting—who bring to life the vision of the designers. Masks and props of all kinds are also made in-house to demanding standards, and virtually all swords and daggers used on stage are real weapons made in the Festival's armoury. This exhibition includes five spectacular costumes worn by Stratford's leading ladies through the years, serving as testament to the exceptional skills of Festival artisans.

These costumes and other items included in this exhibition are part of the Stratford Festival Archives. With more than two thousand costumes, hundreds of props, and 250,000 photographs and videos, as well as extensive artistic, production, and administrative files, it is the largest archive devoted to a single theatre in the world, and a unique and invaluable resource for scholars, students, actors, directors, broadcasters, journalists, and others.

"If this were played upon a stage now, I could condemn it as an improbable fiction" (*Twelfth Night*, Act III, scene 4)

THERE IS LITTLE QUESTION that the thrust stage has influenced and continues to influence acting, directing, and design—indeed every aspect of the Stratford Festival. But where did this remarkable performance space spring from and how did it come to be built in the unlikely setting of a small Ontario town?

Like a Shakespearean plot, the story is familiar yet always engaging. Tom Patterson, a Stratford journalist, was looking for a way to revive the sagging fortunes of his formerly railway-driven hometown and decided in 1951 that the answer was a Shakespearean festival.

The timing was right. That same year, the influential *Royal Commission on National Development in the Arts, Letters & Sciences,* better known as the *Massey Report,* was published, leading to the establishment of the Canada Council for the Arts in 1957. Robertson Davies, who wrote the theatre portion of the *Report,* argued that while Canada had its share of theatrical talent, it was utterly lacking in facilities, training, and professional opportunity.

Interestingly, the *Report* made direct reference to the idea of a Shakespearean festival along the lines of the famous one in England. "If the Shakespeare Memorial Theatre, we were told, could be transplanted bodily from Stratford-on-Avon to Ottawa-on-the-Rideau, with all its equipment, we would still be without a National Theatre; but if we can develop even one company, acting in a tent or in school halls, which can move Canadians to tears and laughter with the great plays of the past, and with great plays of the present, we have the heart of a National Theatre."

Patterson probably had no idea he would be doing exactly that when he began to develop his bold idea for Stratford. He soon connected with the doyenne of Canadian theatre, Dora Mavor Moore. She suggested that the best person to advise the new festival was celebrated British director Tyrone Guthrie. Patterson called Guthrie at his home in Ireland and arranged for him to visit the town in July 1952.

It was more than Patterson's persistence and salesmanship that brought the internationally renowned impresario to little Stratford, Ontario. Guthrie had long been fascinated by the idea of creating a unique space, modelled on the Elizabethan stage, for the performance of Shakespeare. He wanted to break the mould of the proscenium arch theatre, with its conventions and clichés, and create a dynamic and fluid environment that fostered an intimate connection between audience and actors.

In June 1937, he had directed a production of *Hamlet* starring Laurence Olivier at Elsinore in Denmark. The play was intended to be produced outdoors with the castle as a backdrop, but torrential rain drove the performers inside to a hotel ballroom. The audience surrounded the hastily constructed platform on three sides. "I should never have suggested staging this rather important occasion as we did if I had not already had a strong hunch that it would work," Guthrie later wrote. "At its best moments that performance in the ballroom related the audience to a Shakespeare play in a different and, I thought, more logical, satisfactory, and effective way than can ever be achieved in a theatre of what is still regarded as orthodox design." In 1948, Guthrie directed a sixteenth-century Scottish play, *Ane Satire of the Thrie Estaites,* in the Assembly Hall of the Church of Scotland for the Edinburgh Festival. In this unique setting, he created his first thrust stage: a large open platform accessible from three sides, with a gallery across the back. The production was so successful that it was revived in 1949 and 1959, and the Assembly Hall became an important performance space for the Edinburgh Festival.

When first approached informally by Mrs. Mavor Moore, Guthrie saw the potential to realize his dream of doing Shakespeare on a similar stage. "I am intensely interested," he wrote to her, "to produce

Shakespeare on a stage that might reproduce the actor-audience relation for which he wrote … I assume that at Stratford, Ontario … the stage and auditorium are still to be made. And if I could influence their design, I would be very happy to do so." Later he wrote to Patterson, "It would be wise to avoid the usual course of entrusting the eventually functional design of a theatre to the local Borough Surveyor, or a landscape gardener, or worst of all—to a committee."

Guthrie's dream was Patterson's opportunity. At Guthrie's suggestion, Patterson secured the services of Tanya Moiseiwitsch, a gifted English designer who had worked with the famous director on a highly successful production of *Henry VIII* at the Old Vic. "It's now known as my stage, but that's not strictly true," wrote Moiseiwitsch later. "Guthrie knew exactly what he wanted: he drew it on the back of an envelope. …I had to turn it into a half-inch-to-the-foot scale model." In a January 1953 press release, Guthrie was quoted as saying flatly, "There will be no drastic improvement in staging Shakespeare until we return to certain basic conditions of the Shakespearean stage."

Leaving the Clichés Behind

THE STAGE GUTHRIE ENVISIONED and Moiseiwitsch created was influenced both by the Elizabethan stage and the amphitheatres of ancient Greece and Rome. It was a curtainless hexagonal platform with a gutter separating it from the amphitheatre-style seating. A stage balcony was set on the diagonal against the back wall, supported by nine slender pillars. For the first four seasons, this extraordinary performance space was located under a huge blue-grey and rust canvas tent. When the permanent theatre was built in 1957, the stage remained in place, and architect Robert Fairfield created the permanent building around it. The balcony, with its central pillar marking the geographic centre of the structure, held the engineer's tripod used for making all radial measurements.

For those who have grown up with this stage, it is difficult to appreciate how revolutionary it was and how wide its impact. Alec Guinness, the big-name British star who performed in the Festival's first season, pronounced that "picture-frame Shakespeare is finished." Guthrie himself wrote in 1953 that while the stage might undergo modification over time, "of the general plan I have no doubts whatever. With

practice we shall all—directors, designers, and actors—learn to use it more skillfully, forgetting many of the clichés of the proscenium stage." Robertson Davies wrote that the new stage lent a strong sense of ritual to the productions of the first Festival season. "It was the effect of a temple: [the audience was] as necessary to the completeness of what was being done as were the actors and those who stood behind them. We were not spectators; we were part of a great ceremony of evocation and celebration."

Cecil Clarke and Tanya Moiseiwitsch with a model of the thrust stage

An Evolving Space

AS GUTHRIE PREDICTED, the stage has undergone small changes but his concept has remained intact. When the permanent theatre was built in 1956–1957, an underground chamber was created beneath the stage, and a trapdoor entrance was added to the main apron stage. The number of upstage entrances was increased, and an orchestra chamber was created twenty-two feet above and immediately behind the main stage.

The thrust stage in 1982 (top)
and in 1997 (bottom)

The audience arc, with its new balcony, was reduced to 220° from 260°, and the seating, which was increased from 1500 to 2192, was designed so that no member of the audience was more than seventy feet from the stage. In 1962, major changes were made to the stage under the direction of Tanya Moiseiwitsch and designer Brian Jackson. The upstage area was widened and opened up, two small balconies were eliminated, two large panelled entrances were added, and the number of pillars was reduced from nine to five. In a Festival media release, Artistic Director Michael Langham noted that the gender of the stage "has changed from feminine to masculine—more in keeping with the robust nature of most of Shakespeare's works." The contrast between the original and the 1962 stage is brought to life in this exhibition by a full-scale model that shows the two stage balconies side by side.

The next changes came in the mid-seventies, under the artistic directorship of Robin Phillips. The riser under the balcony was eliminated by the addition of a wraparound level running from the upstage right steps to the upstage left steps, the bottom step was enlarged, and a canopy was added to the second level of the balcony. In 1976, the balcony was made removable to provide more flexibility and to open up possibilities for opera, operetta, and musical comedy. Phillips explained, "While it does enhance more robust works of Shakespeare, the balcony has an inherent aggressiveness inimical to the staging of other works." Further alterations were made to the balcony in 1987–1988, making its prow, oak facings, and oak column covers removable, providing even more flexibility. In 1997, under the leadership of Artistic Director Richard Monette, a further renewal took place. The audience arc was changed to 175°, reducing the total number of seats—from 2276 to 1832—and some of the demands on actors; sightlines and acoustics were improved. The exhibition traces this evolution from 1953 to the present through a series of photographs.

Building a National Theatre

TYRONE GUTHRIE'S revolutionary stage design shaped every aspect of the Stratford Festival, helping to give it a place in world theatre. Just as the stage made Stratford, so Stratford has contributed to the development of a vigorous regional theatre industry across Canada.

When the Festival was first proposed, there were those who argued that it would have a negative effect on Canadian theatre, siphoning off the best talent from across the country to play in European classics. Guthrie quickly defended the concept, pointing out that before Stratford, talented young Canadians had to leave their homeland to have viable careers in the theatre.

Almost from the beginning, the Stratford Festival was a force beyond its home in southwestern Ontario. The Canadian Players company was launched after the first season to employ Festival actors during the fall and winter. Tony van Bridge, a long-time member of both companies, notes: "The Canadian Players took theatre to the whole country, to the whole continent, and throughout North America built Canada's reputation for fine classical acting." In the late 1970s, Festival stalwarts Marti Maraden and Nicholas Pennell toured Canada doing two-handed plays and acting workshops. In Vancouver, a reviewer wrote of their made-in-Stratford "Phillips" style as "uncluttered and spare yet rich and eloquent."

By its third season, the Festival had also developed a structured theatre training program and had thirty young actors studying voice and movement. Training continued in various forms, including the famous Young Company established by Robin Phillips in 1975 and revived in various forms by subsequent artistic directors. In 1998, Artistic Director Richard Monette established what is now the Birmingham Conservatory for Classical Theatre Training, which offers learning opportunities to actors and directors.

As one of the first major theatres built in North America in the twentieth century, the Festival theatre marked the beginning of a Canadian construction boom. As Tom Patterson later put it: "For the following two decades, hardly a year went by without another theatre being initiated. During the 1960s and 1970s, every few months another sponsor, architect, or civic official would arrive in Stratford to check out 'How To Do It.'" Between 1957 and 1970, the National Theatre School, the Shaw Festival, the Manitoba Theatre Centre, Neptune Theatre, the Vancouver Playhouse, the Charlottetown Festival, the Citadel, the Globe Theatre, Theatre Calgary, the Centaur, Theatre New Brunswick, and the National Arts Centre were established.

Here are just a few examples of how Stratford has shared its theatrical treasures:

- Tom Patterson, Leon Major (an assistant director at Stratford), and playwright John Gray were commissioned to produce a report on Canadian theatre for the Canada Council in 1961. During their visit to Halifax, Patterson gave a rousing speech about the benefits of a professional theatre for community development. That seed sprouted into the Neptune Theatre.
- After his time at Stratford, Michael Langham went on to work with the Guthrie Theatre in Minneapolis and the Drama Division of the Julliard School of the Arts, and then returned to Canada to help found the Atlantic Theatre Festival in Wolfville, New Brunswick.
- In 1968, young Stratford actor Christopher Newton was recruited to start up a professional theatre in Calgary. Somewhat hesitant, he was encouraged by promises of support from his Festival colleagues. Newton put Theatre Calgary on a firm footing and moved on to new challenges, eventually serving as artistic director of the Shaw Festival for more than twenty years.
- More recently, twelve outstanding Canadian actors came together to create Toronto's Soulpepper Theatre Company. Of the twelve, six had been in Robin Phillips's Young Company, three had been in other young companies, and two more had other Stratford experience.

"The world's my oyster" (*The Merry Wives of Windsor*, Act II, scene 2)

THE THRUST STAGE itself has been copied and adapted in many theatres around the world, including Minneapolis, Dallas, Los Angeles, New York,

Atlanta, Washington, London (Globe Theatre and National Theatre), Chichester, Nottingham, Manchester, Sheffield, and even Moscow. The Rockefeller Foundation sent a delegation to Stratford to take measurements and study seat angles in preparation for designing the Beaumont Theatre at the Lincoln Centre in New York City.

Recently the Royal Shakespeare Company announced that it is remaking its theatre. Representatives visited the Stratford Festival, borrowing blueprints and photos of its famous stage. In June 2006, Artistic Director Michael Boyd explained the changes. "We want to move away from the nineteenth-century proscenium 'picture frame' to a theatre that embraces interaction," he said. "Our commitment to bring an immediacy and clarity to Shakespeare means we need to bring the audience to a more engaged relationship with our actors. The best way we can achieve this is in a bold thrust stage, a modern take on the theatres of Shakespeare's day." It could almost be Guthrie talking to Stratford City Council more than fifty years ago.

Tom Patterson and Tyrone Guthrie came together at an auspicious moment in Canadian theatre history, and the result was the Stratford Festival of Canada. Would it be what it is today without Guthrie's revolutionary vision and Moiseiwitsch's design for a bold thrust stage? Would its impact have been felt across Canada and around the world? Antoni Cimolino, the Festival's general director, puts it simply: "That stage was the whole reason we happened."

Pat Morden attended the University of Western Ontario and then completed a Masters in history at the University of Sussex as a Commonwealth Scholar. After several years as a freelance magazine writer, she was hired as editor of the Western Alumni Gazette and manager of alumni communications at Western. In 1994, she and her partner Max started Morden Communications. Since then, the company has received more than twenty local, national, and international awards for their work, including an International Association of Business Communicators Gold Quill award.

| DJANET SEARS

notes of a coloured girl:
32 short reasons why i write
for the theatre

1 Carved from that same tree
in another age
counsel/warriors who
in the mother tongue
made drums talk
now in another tongue
make words to walk in rhythm
'cross the printed page
carved from that same tree
in another age
—Khephra [1]

2 Nearly a decade ago I found myself speaking with es-
teemed writer and Nobel laureate Derek Walcott about
an upcoming staged reading I was directing of his play
A Branch of the Blue Nile. Toward the end of our conversation I politely requested an opportunity to ask him
what I termed a stupid question. His eyebrows seemed
to crawl up to his hairline, but he didn't say no. Not that
I gave him a chance. Swiftly managing to kick all second
thoughts out of my mind, I boldly asked him to tell me

Sears's adaptation of *Othello*, *Harlem Duet*, is notable for many reasons, not the least of which is that it is the first play by a Black Canadian playwright to have won a Governor General's Literary Award and the first all-Black play to be staged at the Stratford Festival. Sears's play is prefaced by *notes of a coloured girl: 32 short reasons why i write for the theatre*, which eloquently addresses issues of diversity in Canadian theatre and the motivations that prompted her to write this adaptation. Sears's words speak to the challenges of pluralism and cultural diversity that find expression in contemporary Canadian adaptations of Shakespeare. *32 short reasons* provides compelling insight into the sources, cultural, artistic, and otherwise, from which the power of adaptation flows, as well as into the power of theatre as a form of community expression.

LEFT Astrid Janson, costume design for Othello in *Harlem Duet* (2006) why he wrote. He retreated to the back of his seat, and after several long moments of pondering, he replied, "I don't know." He said that writing wasn't really a choice for him. From as far back as he could recall, he had written. He described it as a type of organic urge. He didn't know why he wrote, but when he experienced this urge, he felt compelled to act on it. Be it on a plane, first thing in the morning, or last thing at night.

3 From as far back as I can recall, I never believed in miracles. My life had taught me not to. Then I witnessed the birth of my sister's first baby. I'd seen birth films. I'd even studied human reproduction at the undergraduate level. But this child came out of my sister—already alive. I mean, not yet fully born, her head alone protruding from between her mother's thighs, she wailed. Full of voice, she slipped out of the velvety darkness that was her mother's womb, into the light. I was overcome. I watched as Qwyn, this tiny, golden-umber-coloured soul, caught by an opaque-rubber-gloved doctor in a white coat, was separated from the placenta and bundled into blanched cloth. I stood there for a moment and wondered how she would come to know of herself, blinded by the glare of snow? What would this fair world tell her? I experienced such a sadness for her—or maybe it was for myself.

4 I wanted there to be no question of her right to take up space on the planet.

5 I was already eighteen when I saw Ntozake Shange's *For Coloured Girls Who Have Considered Suicide When the Rainbow is Enuf* in New York City. This was the first live stage production by a writer of African descent I had ever seen. **6** This will not be Qwyn's fate (nor the fate of her younger sister Kyla, her cousins VaNessah, Djustice, Ariane, Justin, Donny, Sherie, or Danielle). **7** They must have access to a choir of African voices, chanting a multiplicity of African experiences. One voice does not a chorus make. And I will not wait. **8** I harbour deep within me tales that I've never told. **9** I too must become an organ and add my perspective, my lens, my stories, to the ever-growing body of work by and about people of African descent.

10 Forty-seven years ago, and nine months before I was born, in a country over three thousand miles away, Lorraine Hansberry began rehearsals for her first play. In the season of my birth, *A Raisin in the Sun* opened to extraordinary critical and popular acclaim.

11 *A Raisin in the Sun* marked a turning point, for until this time no Black writer, Black actor, Black director, or technician had benefited financially from any of the plays about Black people that had been presented [in the commercial theatre].[2]

12 An old West African proverb states that, as a people, we stand on the shoulders of our ancestors. **13** Lorraine Hansberry is my mother—in the theatre—and she accompanies me wherever I go. **14** I have been known to drop her a few lines, now and then. **15** Yes, she responds. **16** As a woman of African descent and a writer for the stage, I stand on her shoulders. They are a firm and formidable foundation on which to rest my large and awkward feet.

17 Acting is a craft that I have been called to by my nature. Writing is a craft that I have chosen to nurture. **18** As a young actor, I soon realized that a majority of the roles that I would be offered did not portray me in the way I saw myself, my family, or my friends, in life. I became consumed by my own complaining. **19** Complaining, imploring, and protesting, only served to disperse my energy.

20 Protest takes an enormous toll. We can and should make noise. However, in most cases our screams fall upon deaf ears.

21 Don't get me wrong here, without protest we'd never have had the likes of Martin, Malcolm, or Angela. Activism is a craft in and of itself. My skills are as a theatre practitioner, and this is the medium I must use.

That's why I am so impressed by artists like Baraka, Sanchez, Bullins, Caldwell, Hansberry, Baldwin, Giovanni, Milner, and Ahmed, many of whom were involved in the Black Arts Movement of the 1960s. The fact is they used their work as a vehicle with which to express personal and political passions.

22 In early 1993, Christine Moynihan approached me, on behalf of the Toronto Theatre Alliance and Equity Showcase Productions, about co-ordinating the spring "Loon Café"—a one-off evening of presentations involving a host of performers, directors, writers, production workers, designers, and supporters. I agreed, on the condition that I could do anything. In the ensuing weeks, I developed the blueprint for the evening, which I titled: *Negrophilia: An African American Retrospective: 1959–1971.* The three studio spaces of Equity Showcase were renamed: Obsidian, Onyx, and Jet. And the events taking place, three in each room over the course of the evening, involved readings, performances, and discussions around Black theatre in America. There were plays that I had loved and only read. One new piece, *Jimmy and Lolo,* was a collaboration based on an idea that had been brewing inside of me for ages. Performed on the rooftop of an adjacent building, the play tells the story of the relationship between James Baldwin and Lorraine Hansberry. The entire event was inspirational; a rousing celebration of Blackness.

23 I have a dream. A dream that one day in the city where I live, at any given time of the year, I will be able to find at least one play that is filled with people that look like me, telling stories about me, my family, my friends, my community. For most people of European descent, this is a privilege taken for granted.

24 Like Derek Walcott, I too have no choice. I must write my own work for the theatre. I must produce my own work and the work of other writers of African descent. Then Qwyn's, her sister's, and their cousins' experiences of this world will almost certainly be different from my own.

25 But where do I start? How do I find the words?

26 My good friend Clarissa Chandler, a business consultant, educator, and motivational speaker, shared with me a process for using my nagging mind and my raging heart as a way to get back in touch with my innermost knowing and creative desires. She identified three steps of transformation that I could use like footprints leading me back home.

27 First: identify the place of complaint. (This can sometimes be evident in the complaining we do in hiding, in conversation with friends, and/or in the privacy of our own minds.) Second: Say it out loud. Create a mantra out of it. (Give it room in the world). Third: locate a creative point of expression for this mantra. **28** Paint it, dance it, sculpt it, or write about it. Why limit yourself?

29 As a veteran theatre practitioner of African descent, Shakespeare's Othello had haunted me since I first was introduced to him. Sir Laurence Olivier in blackface. Othello is the first African portrayed in the annals of western dramatic literature. In an effort to exorcise this ghost, I have written *Harlem Duet. Harlem Duet,* a rhapsodic blues tragedy, explores the effects of race and sex on the lives of people of African descent. It is a tale of love. The tale of Othello and his first wife Billie. Set in 1860, 1928, and contemporary Harlem at the corner of Malcolm X and Martin Luther King Boulevards (125th Street and Lennox Avenue), this is Billie's story. The exorcism begins.

30 For the many like me, Black and female, it is imperative that our writing begin to recreate our histories and our myths, as well as to integrate the most painful of experiences. [3] Writing for me is a labour of love, probably not unlike the experience of giving birth. In a very deep way, I feel that I am in the process of giving birth to myself. Writing for the stage allows me a process to dream myself into existence.

31 In a recent clinical study at Duke University, researchers found that racist comments can not only lead directly to an overworked heart, but the internal stress caused by racism was found to tear the lining of blood vessels. [4] I must write to save my own life.

32 There are a great many times when I forget. I forget why I'm doing this. Days when the blues move from a deep cerulean to icy cold pale. So I have the following words by Langston Hughes on my wall, just above my desk, for those times when I most need reminding.

SOMEDAY SOMEBODY'LL
STAND UP AND TALK ABOUT ME
AND WRITE ABOUT ME—
BLACK AND BEAUTIFUL
AND SING ABOUT ME,
AND PUT ON PLAYS ABOUT ME!
I RECKON IT'LL BE
ME MYSELF!
YES, IT'LL BE ME.
—Langston Hughes [5]

ENDNOTES

1 Khephra, "Talking Drums #1," *Essence Magazine,* March, 1990, 125.

2 Woodie King and Ron Milner, eds., "Evolution of a People's Theatre," *Black Drama Anthology* (New York: Signet, 1971), vii.

3 Marlene Philip, *She Tries Her Tongue* (Charlottetown, PEI: Ragweed Press, 1989), 25.

4 Deborah Franklin, Sally Lehrman, and Michael Mason, "Vital Signs: Racism Hurts the Heart Twice," *Health* (October, 1996), 24.

5 Langston Hughes, "Note on Commercial Theatre," *Selected Poems Langston Hughes* (New York: Random House, Inc., 1974), 190.

Djanet Sears is a playwright, actor, and director. Born to a Guyanese father and a Jamaican mother, Sears was raised in England and in Saskatoon, Saskatchewan. Her birth name was Janet—she added the "D" when she came across a town called Djanet on a trip to Africa. She has won many awards for her play *Harlem Duet*, including four Dora Mavor Moore Awards and a Governor General's Award for drama. Sears is a founding member of Obsidian Theatre, a Toronto theatre company that specializes in African and Caribbean Canadian drama. She is also a professor at the University of Toronto.

Possible Worlds—
Designing for Shakespeare in Canada

THE POSSIBLE WORLDS component of the Shakespeare—Made in Canada exhibition throws light on Canadian productions of Shakespearean plays from the point of view of theatrical designers. The theatrical works exhibited in the gallery span several decades and represent a wide range of venues and artists from across the country. The designs derive from the L. W. Conolly Theatre Archives at the University of Guelph— the largest archive on Canadian theatre in Canada—and from the Macdonald Stewart Art Centre's collection, augmented by works from the Canadian Theatre Museum, the Stratford Festival Archives, and private collections.

As a professional theatre designer and a professor in the School of English and Theatre Studies at the University of Guelph, I have long felt the need to promote and encourage understanding of theatrical design as an art form in its own right. Initially, I had intended to focus my research on design collections contained in archives across the country with particular emphasis on the theatre collection at the University of Guelph in order to give proper attention to this relatively new field of study. Collaboration with the Canadian Adaptations of Shakespeare Project (CASP) has broadened the range of my inquiries to a reflection on the adaptive nature of this art form.

Shakespeare's work is unique in that his staggeringly broad understanding of humanity lends itself so readily to various interpretations—

what some might call adaptations—that fit local, regional, and national contexts. By its very nature, theatrical design is adaptive: directors and designers synthesize external influences to create the world of the play, tailoring their research to suit the concept of a particular production. The visual aspects of any theatrical production are central to communicating an adaptive context; this exhibition illustrates how these elements come together in a completed work of art.

It also represents the initial stages in an exploration that asks how we communicate our understanding of the world to our contemporaries: Are we merely the by-product of our colonial heritage? Are we developing our own Canadian ways of interpreting theatre and the works of Shakespeare in particular? Are we finally moving beyond the past to acknowledge our multicultural reality in the creation of a uniquely Canadian vision?

Our Colonial Past

IT IS IMPORTANT to situate a discussion of Canadian theatrical design in relation to its time. Attitudes toward theatre artists, specifically designers, have changed considerably since the early years of theatrical production in Canada. This is, in part, because the notion of assigning responsibility for the creation of the visual aspects of a play to one individual is a modern concept. Early "theatricals" of the eighteenth century would have had rudimentary scenery and costumes produced by anyone who was handy with a hammer or a needle and thread. It wasn't until the late nineteenth century that a need for an artist to create a cohesive visual interpretation of the play script was recognized in Europe. Consequently, it is extremely difficult to find any record of stage designs or designers for any of Canada's early theatre productions.

The production of plays in Canada dates back to the days of the early colonists. In fact, performances of plays by British authors, Shakespeare in particular, could be viewed as a form of cultural imperialism. In 1759, after General Wolfe defeated Marquis de Montcalm on the Plains of Abraham, the British needed to take control of the many towns built around the military garrisons that had been established by the French. Amateur theatre, usually performed by members of the British military, featured the work of playwrights such as Shakespeare. It was only natural that the large majority of new settlers from the British Isles would embrace the ideal of the theatre they knew from home and would wish to produce the works of great British playwrights. But the British also realized that power lay in the hands of those able to dominate this new land, culturally as well as physically.

The legacy of this domination continues today: witness the predominance of a British model of theatrical practice in Canada. Our position as an English colony meant that touring productions by professional British actors, directors, and designers dominated our theatres until the Great War. Canadian theatre artists, particularly designers, only began to work as professionals in the 1940s. This colonial heritage was formative in the early development of theatre artists in Canada. Inevitably, it was essential to overcome, if not critique and revise, this colonial inheritance in order to change perceptions and enable the creation of a distinctively Canadian theatre—a theatre that told our stories through playwrights, directors, and artists who both created their own work and reimagined the works of European writers, such as Shakespeare, from their own perspectives.

Guelph-born artist Rolph Scarlett (1889–1984), the earliest designer represented here, would have found very little training or opportunity as an aspiring designer in Canada in the 1920s; consequently, he chose to live and work in the United States. The circumstances of the Canadian theatre world would have been somewhat better for Herbert Whittaker (1910–2006). Whittaker was fortunate to have worked with the Canadian Players, one of the first and most influential theatre companies of post-World War II Canada. Unlike the theatrical touring companies from Britain and the United States that were the norm in the early part of the century, the Canadian Players, founded in 1954, was made up primarily of actors, directors, and designers who had made the commitment to live and work in Canada. Senior members of this company were sometimes born and trained overseas, but they wished to create theatre as Canadians, thus giving aspiring artists the chance to work and learn in their own country.

The Canadian Players and companies like it made creative theatrical work in Canada viable from both economic and aesthetic points of view. Colonial artists could not only produce their own work, but they could build on the background of their British predecessors and create a unique vision of theatre as a function of local, regional, and national realities. Canadian Players gave many of our most prominent actors their start in a company that toured throughout North America. For example, Whittaker's 1961 design for the Canadian Players production of *King Lear* is historically important in its attempt to forge a distinctly Canadian adaptation through the use of images we recognize as part of our world—far removed from Shakespeare's Britain. Whittaker was an important figure from the formative years of Canadian theatre; his large body of work can be seen at the Canadian Theatre Museum, which he established.

Even as late as the 1980s, many Canadians viewed themselves as colonial offspring of the British Empire. It was still believed that artists of any significance in Canada had to be born in or, at the very least, educated in the United Kingdom. Only recently, we've crawled out from under this largely self-imposed colonial mentality to assert ourselves and develop as theatre artists in our own right. This shift in attitude has applied particularly to Canadian designers of Shakespeare, but of a Shakespeare remade in Canada.

Sir Tyrone Guthrie (1900–1971), the eminent Shakespearean director from the Old Vic Theatre in London, England, was invited in 1953 to Canada to establish the Stratford Shakespearean Festival. He brought with him Tanya Moiseiwitsch, a young British designer of Russian descent, to design the innovative, highly influential thrust stage, and to establish a design tradition that permeates the work of many contemporary Canadian theatre designers across the country. We owe a great debt to the talent and generosity of British designers like Moiseiwitsch, Desmond Heeley, and Leslie Hurry, three of Stratford's early designers, who each shared their knowledge, trained many Canadians, and set the high standard of design that is practiced today. It is ironic, however, that this benevolent presence at one of our two major theatre festivals further reinforced the perception that only foreign, preferably British-trained designers could design for Shakespeare, who was, after all, the epitome of British cultural achievement.

Susan Benson, whose evocative designs for *Romeo and Juliet* appear in this exhibition, has made a significant contribution to changing this attitude. Born in England in 1942, she recently celebrated forty years of living and working in Canada. As head of design at the Stratford Festival from 1980 to 1983, she established an apprenticeship program to train and encourage Canadian designers to work as equals with the international artists at the Festival. Three designers in this exhibition— Patrick

Clark, Charlotte Dean, and John Pennoyer—have all benefited from this program. Canadian designers now share the stage at Stratford on an equal footing with their international counterparts.

"Myself in different circumstances:" The Ephemera of Design Aesthetics

THEATRICAL DESIGN IS often ignored as an art form, possibly due to its collaborative nature and the fact that it often references the work of other visual artists—painters, sculptors, and so on—in its execution. Collaborative work has long been recognized in the art world. Few would question the artistic merit of teams like Christo and Jeanne Claude, for example, whose collaborative environmental installations such as the wrapping of the Pont Neuf in Paris or the recent *Gates* project in New York's Central Park have been recognized as innovative artistic achievements. In contrast, theatrical design is often thought of simply as an elaboration of a director's ideas or as a technical solution to a problem, rather than as artistic vision.

Designers are, in fact, visual directors whose work, at its best, supports the work of actors and clarifies the playwright's text through the languages of colour, light, proportion, and dimension. Theatrical designers approach their work through careful analysis of a play text and, when possible, through collaboration with the director and playwright, arriving at a visual interpretation of the images and metaphors of the script. These images are sometimes inspired by the work of other artists, reinterpreted through the designer's own vision of the world of the play. A designer collaborates further with actors and technicians in the realization of this vision since the ultimate goal is not to create a static image, but to breathe life into the world of the play. This rendition of a play script is one of the most important possible avenues for generating an adaptive context that brings together a particular production's vision with the playwright's words. Set renderings, models, and costume sketches are a mid-point in this process, not the culmination of the work.

A theatrical design exists on two levels: the rendering, where the designer's skill in creating a discrete work of art can be appreciated in its own right; and the design itself. This second level is at the core of a designer's art. It is subtle as it deals with the creation of fleeting moments in time and space—ephemeral conceptualizations that are much harder to understand, appreciate, and document.

I have borrowed the title for this portion of the Shakespeare—Made in Canada exhibition from the play *Possible Worlds* by John Mighton, winner of the 2005 Siminovitch Prize in Theatre for his contribution to Canadian playwriting. "Possible Worlds" so aptly describes the design work represented in this exhibition. The actor William Hutt, in conversation, has described one of his approaches to acting as "myself in different circumstances." These changing circumstances are also a designer's currency as they create possible worlds onstage. The Possible Worlds gallery, then, attempts to illustrate the high level of imagination and creativity Canadian designers bring to their work as it relates to Shakespearean productions. It also explores the many possible visual responses to one text. These responses are often a reflection of the times and contexts in which the work was staged.

It is important to preserve and archive the work of designers. Since the nineteenth century, photographic records of productions have been the primary source of information about specific design and directorial interpretations of a play; they have also served as a visual record of theatrical movements or schools of thought. How different to read the staging ideas of the great Russian theatrical innovator Constantine Stanislavski (1863–1938), for example, then to see the "realism" of his mise en scène which seems very artificial to modern eyes and far from the ideal he describes in his writings.

Archived designer drawings and production photographs are a window into the past. They are not the production itself, but these artifacts do recall and evoke the evanescent world that was created far better than words alone can describe; they allow the viewer to make his or her own conclusions—to imagine what might have actually taken place in a particular setting. But, as this exhibition shows, theatrical designs also stand alone as creative work in their own right.

Intercultural Design: The Canadian Multicultural Context

MUCH HAS CHANGED in Canada's cultural make-up over the years. Theatre in Canada has grown from the British tradition to embrace the influences of a much larger cultural mosaic. Astrid Janson's work on *Harlem Duet,* seen in this exhibition, is an example of an adaptation of Shakespeare that arises from another cultural tradition. Janson is a Canadian of German descent working with an all-Black company on a play inspired by *Othello.* It is, in many ways, a typical Canadian multicultural convergence, inspired by Shakespeare yet adapted to a specifically Canadian context that addresses issues of diversity.

Cameron Porteous, whose designs for *King Lear* and *Twelfth Night* appear here, has done significant work to open our eyes to the perspective of countries such as Germany, Poland, Russia, and the Czech Republic. As head of design at the Shaw Festival in Niagara-on-the-Lake from 1980 to 1997, he invited European designers to the Festival and promoted the exchange of ideas

Production photograph from *King Lear* (Canadian Players Tour, 1961–1962)

between Canadian and European theatre artists. He recognized the need to look beyond our established traditions and ways of working to explore new directions in and attitudes toward production. The result has been an attitudinal shift that has opened our eyes to European scenography and to a multicultural and intercultural world that more closely reflects contemporary Canada.

My starting point for imagining this exhibition was a photograph that showed William Hutt as King Lear in Inuit costuming. Fascinated by the photograph, I sought out the original designs by long-time *Globe and Mail* theatre critic and designer Herbert Whittaker, whose importance to twentieth-century Canadian theatre has already been mentioned. One of the challenges of designing *King Lear* is to create a believable world where the extreme events of the play can take place. Whittaker writes on the back of one of his drawings:

> In 1946, David Gardner invited me to design the two plays for The Canadian Players Tour he was to direct— *King Lear* and *The Lady's Not For Burning,* to star William Hutt. We agreed that the primitive society Canadians recognized best was not Early Britain's but our own Eskimo Tradition: So grew "The Eskimo Lear."

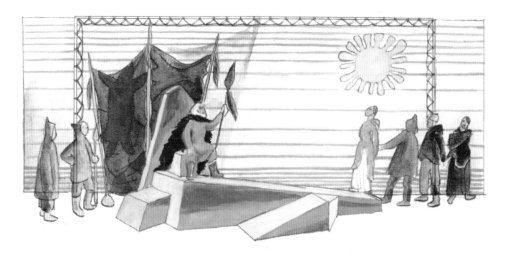

CANADIAN PLAYERS: "KING LEAR"   Herbert Whittaker. Aug.1961

This Canadian Players production of *King Lear* was heralded as a uniquely Canadian interpretation because it used imagery from a culture that was part of the "Great White North"—images of a supposedly "primitive" culture, then assumed to be within the purview of a Canadian sensibility. Although it may now be seen as a form of cultural appropriation, this production was created at a time of new awareness and curiosity about the peoples of northern Canada, a time when the art of the Inuit was still unknown to a majority of North Americans. Whittaker's "Eskimo Lear" was, in its own way, revolutionary in its attempt to shed light on this world. The set for the production makes use of a distinctly theatrical style of representation. This was partly dictated by its function as a touring set, which had to be assembled and taken down easily while the Canadian Players toured through Canada and the United States. In the performance space, Whittaker's abstracted iceberg-like designs would also have brought to mind the northern landscape of Canada as seen through the eyes of Group of Seven painter Lawren Harris (1885–1970).

Patrick Clark, costume design for *King Lear* (Stratford Festival, 1996)

LEFT Herbert Whittaker, set design for *King Lear* (Canadian Players Tour, 1961–1962)

Rolph Scarlett, set design for *King Lear* (1928)

As we will see in other examples, the notion of creating a design through the appropriation, reinterpretation and, sometimes, misuse of visual images from another culture is not uncommon when designers and directors seek a means of presentation that will clarify the text to a varied audience.

Compare the image of the "Eskimo Lear" to Rolph Scarlett's 1928 designs for *King Lear*. In addition to designing for the theatre, Scarlett was an abstract painter, an industrial designer, and a noted jeweller. His designs for *King Lear* show the influence of the great theatre theorist and director Edward Gordon Craig (1872–1966). Scarlett's design aesthetic is reductive, the performers dwarfed by staging that relies on the use of light and movement to express the themes of the play.

Consider also Patrick Clark's 1996 design of *King Lear* at the Stratford Festival, once again starring Hutt as Lear. The original concept had the play set in the Edwardian period, but Clark suggested a change to England of the 1880s. As he puts it, "I just couldn't see those nice Edwardian ladies doing all those horrible things and it seemed to me that a darker, industrialized world made so much more of the play understandable. The shapes of the 1880s are also sexier and allow the women in the play to have strength as well as a sensuousness that was essential for their characters."[1]

Charlotte Dean, costume design for *King Lear* (Necessary Angel Theatre Company, 1995)

There are two more interpretations of *King Lear* for further comparison in this exhibition: Cameron Porteous's costume design for Powys Thomas as Lear at the Vancouver Playhouse (1976); and Charlotte Dean's designs for a non-gender-specific version directed by Richard Rose for Toronto's Necessary Angel Theatre Company (1995). Over the years several great Canadians have played King Lear and Welsh-born Thomas, a veteran Canadian actor and co-founder of the National Theatre School, was renowned for his acting ability. He died in 1977, shortly after this production of *Lear,* but designs and photographs survive to honour his memory.

Charlotte Dean's production of *King Lear* is set in a non-specific northern climate with rigid moral structures. It was influenced by research into both early First Nations American and early European cultures. The combination of cassock shapes and fur over-garments was inspired by the paintings of Quebec artist Jean-Paul Lemieux (1904-1990), known for his abstracted, archetypal figures standing in harsh, northern landscapes. Dean's design was further informed by the Royal Ontario Museum's publication of works from its collection entitled *Cut My Cote*—an important reference on the historical manufacture of garments. A third major influence was the multi-faceted cultural experience of Canada itself—from the Québécois Roman Catholic church, to downtown Toronto's army surplus stores, to Winnipeg's Fur Exchange where Native and European cultures have been conducting commerce for over three hundred years.

Dean's early work as a dyer and painter informed the method of creating both sketches and costumes. The sketches are collages of rice paper, using the same dyes later used to colour the cloth and chamois skins for the actual costumes. The furs were a combination of purchased pelts and second-hand coats from thrift shops across Toronto. The play began with a large banquet scene where all of the characters appeared in their furred regalia, including headdresses, capes, and cassocks. By the time Lear—played by actress Janet Wright of *Corner Gas* fame—appeared on the heath, all of her protective furs were stripped away leaving only animal hide for her clothing, thus underscoring the raw emotion and the fight for survival so integral to the play's progression.

Dean's drawings for *A Midsummer Night's Dream,* produced by the Canadian Stage company in 1995 and 1996, again made use of dyed rice paper; in this case, the garments and props were rendered in a more traditional graphic form, influenced by both Dutch-born classicist painter Sir Lawrence Alma-Tadema and sixteenth-century Flemish artist Pieter Bruegel the Elder. The work of these two artists was reimagined in the pastoral setting of Toronto's High Park where the play was performed outdoors, framed by two massive oaks and with a soundtrack augmented by live crickets, tree frogs, and dogs.

Charlotte Dean, costume design for *A Midsummer Night's Dream* (Canstage, 1995–1996)

Other examples of contrastive designs are represented in three versions of *Twelfth Night:* one by John Pennoyer at the Stratford Festival (2006) and two by Cameron Porteous, produced at the Vancouver Playhouse (1979) and the Citadel Theatre in Edmonton (1999), respectively. Pennoyer and Leon Rubin, a British director who has worked frequently at the Stratford Festival, saw the world of Illyria as an orientalized land where the dialogue and behaviour remained very English. They chose to set the play in nineteenth-century India during the Raj, the time of the British occupation. As with the example of Whittaker's "Eskimo Lear," the appropriation of the culture of an exotic "other" becomes a problematic context for gaining a perspective on our own so-

John Pennoyer, costume
designs for *Twelfth Night*
(Stratford Festival, 2006)

ciety, as one colony's interpretation of Shakespeare relies on another colonial situation for the basis of its design. The irony of this situation—in which colonial influences in a colonial setting produce further colonizing gestures—is perhaps also characteristic of Canadian theatre as it works through its own history toward more decolonized models of theatrical expression.

Masked Identities / Spectral Worlds

THE L. W. CONOLLY Theatre Archives at the University of Guelph is fortunate to have a significant number of designs by Cameron Porteous. A large amount of work in this collection was created during his extensive time as resident designer at the Shaw Festival in Niagara-on-the-Lake (1980–1997). His work is represented in this exhibition by costume renderings, set models, and maquettes of two of Shakespeare's plays.

In the 1979 Vancouver Playhouse version of *Twelfth Night,* Porteous and director Derek Goldby set the play in eighteenth-century Venice, a carnivalesque world well-suited to the sense of intrigue integral to the play. Inspired by a silver-framed mirror given to him by the director, Porteous designed a set made entirely of reflective surfaces, creating a "now you see it, now you don't" world of masked identities and illusion. (The Plexiglas for the set was recycled from a structure built for a United Nations conference on world housing that was held in

Vancouver at the time the play was in rehearsal.) The set model for this production no longer exists, but the costume designs survive to illustrate the intriguing, spectral world that Porteous created.

Prior to designing the Citadel's *Twelfth Night,* Porteous found himself designing a film in Croatia on the shores of the Adriatic Sea. Here, he realized that the mythical world of Illyria was, in fact, a real Croatian province. In the towns in this area, houses rose up the sides of the steep cliffs that ran down into the Adriatic. Ships frequently crashed on these cliffs, as does the ship carrying Viola and her brother Sebastian at the start of *Twelfth Night.* His set design, which can be seen in maquette form, was further inspired by the work of an unnamed Croatian artist who created miniature towns out of stacked boxes. Imagine Sebastian climbing the boxes to Olivia's balcony or hiding in the drawers to spy on Malvolio. Look closely at the maquette, see the fountain containing a model boat at centre stage. The play opened with a spotlight on this model boat as it tossed on the stormy seas of the fountain, eventually shipwrecking. The lights faded to black and came up again on an overturned full-sized rowboat. Characters appeared from under the rowboat to begin the play.

Cameron Porteous, costume designs for *Twelfth Night* (Vancouver Playhouse, 1979)

Emotional Realism: The Poetic Power of the Visual

DANY LYNE'S SET MODELS for *Henry V* at the Stratford Festival (2001) and
for Verdi's adaptation of *Macbeth* at the Canadian Opera Company (2005)
offer another point of comparison. Lyne was born in Montreal but developed an interest in theatre and opera in Toronto. She explains:

> I think it is my interest in opera (a less realistic theatrical
> medium than theatre) and my love of metaphors that has
> led me to a non-realistic design approach. I studied with
> Dr. Paul Baker, an English scholar who focused his atten-
> tion on text analysis. The poetry and images in the texts
> we studied, coupled with the fact that I was a fine arts
> student with a major in painting, inspired me to explore
> an imagistic approach from the onset. More recently, the
> work I saw in Berlin theatre informed my imagination
> and pushed my vision of an emotionally-charged theatre
> closer to an image-based theatre. I often refer to my work
> as emotional realism. [2]

Lyne's design for *Macbeth* takes the form of a minimal yet evocative
set that expresses the emotional reality of the text: the set changes
colour and shape in response to the inner lives of the characters; blood
runs from its walls. Lyne's model for *Macbeth* is accompanied by a sto-
ryboard that shows selected scenes as the designer envisioned them

80

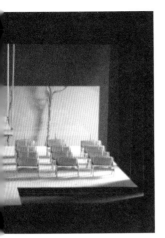

changing through space and time. As mentioned earlier, the design for a performance is not a static creation. The concern for the performance, not mere decoration, is the starting point of a design. Designers must think creatively of the interaction among performers, light, and space as the world of the play unfolds. Storyboarding scenes from a play—a process adapted from film and television production—is becoming a more and more popular way for designers to express their vision, to demonstrate to director, cast, and technical crew how a set will change throughout a production.

By understanding the profound power of an actor in an empty space, designers can enhance a production by simplifying their design, leaving room for the audience to participate actively by using imagination to "fill in the blanks." Teresa Przybylski's *Comedy of Errors*, designed for the Tom Patterson theatre at the Stratford Festival (1994), is a good example of this approach. Constructed of simple frames placed in strategic locations, the set is so minimal that it seems hardly there at all. Yet director Richard Rose and the actors used these simple structures to conjure rooms, walls, and doors so effectively that at one point in the production, when an actor was pushed through a frame that had previously represented a wall, the audience gasped. Designers are pleased to be complemented on the look of a design, but their real success is in the creation of a believable world in the minds of the audience.

Przybylski immigrated to Canada from Poland and currently teaches in the theatre department at York University. Przybylski's approach to

Teresa Przybylski, costume
design for *The Comedy of Errors*
(Stratford Festival, 1994)

RIGHT Susan Benson, costume
design for *Romeo and Juliet*
(The National Ballet of Canada,
1994)

theatre design is based in the Polish theatre tradition, a valuable intercultural addition to the Canadian perspective in counterpoint to a historically English directive. Her costume sketches are particularly fascinating as they depart from a realistic style of rendering. The British tradition grew out of nineteenth-century realistic movement focused on the importance of the text, interpreted by the actor at the centre of the play; other European cultures, including French and German, have a less reverential attitude towards the text and have evolved a "theatre of images" that is more open to the poetic power of the visual. This approach can also be seen in the work of many French Canadian designers.

Among Canada's most prominent designers is Susan Benson. Her design for the National Ballet's *Romeo and Juliet,* remounted in 2006 for the National Ballet of China in Beijing, creates a disturbing world for the star-crossed lovers. Benson designed the ballet at the time of the war in the former Yugoslavia. She was reminded of how history repeats itself by the story of a young couple of differing religions who were killed in Sarajevo. Benson reflected this dangerous atmosphere by layering time periods and showing the disintegration of material goods over time. She states:

> The set treatment was also influenced by how I did the costume designs, where I used black ink dribbled on to water to achieve the backgrounds. I always tend to design the costumes first and then create the world around the people. The music is not pretty—it is wonderful but quite dark, gritty, and disturbing. It was written in the same period as Picasso and Georges Braque. I wanted an asymmetry to the set reflecting the music, but it was pretty difficult to achieve with the needs of the choreography. I deliberately went for a lot of black for the grittiness.
>
> The asymmetrical aspect that I felt in the music, I used in the diagonals that are in the dyeing of the costumes. It also reflected the heraldic influences on costumes of the period but in an abstracted way.

National Ballet of Canada
Romeo and Juliet
Juliet Ball

Juliet is the butterfly caught in the web of darkness, and Romeo has the same sort of innocence, shown in their colours and textures. I always think of the Capulets being the stronger and more menacing group, and the Montagues perhaps being more earthy and closer to the people in their colours. The Montagues, texture—wools—and the Capulets, leathers and velvets—more ornate fabrics. Their colours are in the red / gold / black range. The Montagues are in the green / grey range.

The gypsies, Carnival King, and clowns are the exceptions, as they are all these colours but in a more vibrant range—but never pure contemporary primary colours. There is always an edge to them that tips them away from this. Black is the link between all these groups either as bindings, linings, or under layers—like the black lines and backgrounds in the costume designs. The people of the town are neutral in their colours, a more natural palette, and the fabrics are more homespun and textured. More colour is added in the carnival by straw, autumn flowers in headpieces, rosettes, and diagonal sashes. [3]

Benson used colors and form to express the poetic power of Shakespeare's story. In addition to designing for the theatre, she is a member of the Royal Canadian Academy of Art and is an accomplished painter who has created portraits of many famous Canadian actors. Her practice of designing costumes before the set, using character development as the foundation of the onstage world she is creating, reflects her attentiveness to the role of the actor. The relationship between character development and design aesthetic is palpable in Benson's productions. Benson's conceptual method is somewhat unorthodox; many designers begin creating the world of the play by first designing the physical setting.

Crossing Cultures

ASTRID JANSON'S DESIGN for the 2006 Stratford Festival version of *Harlem Duet,* an adaptation of *Othello,* is the only work included in the exhibition that is set in a contemporary time period. It is also the production that most aptly reflects the process of Shakespearean adaptation by Canadian artists. Written by Djanet Sears, a Canadian playwright and a Governor General's Literary Award winner, *Harlem Duet* is set in Harlem— "the Soweto of America," according to Winnie Mandela—and, perhaps not co-incidentally, features a hopeful yet flawed character named Canada. The 2006 production was the first all-Black play produced at Stratford.

Sears states that she used Shakespeare's *Othello*, influenced by an early memory of Laurence Olivier in blackface, as a departure point for the creation of a prequel to *Othello*, one that challenges societal status quo and encourages people to consider Black perspectives. Conscious thematic choices have been made in order to encourage people to examine their preconceptions of race and racism. *Harlem Duet* signifies changing times in a Canadian

Astrid Janson, costume sketch for *Harlem Duet* (2006)

theatre practice that has not always embraced diversity or respected difference. Just as Canadian designers have struggled to have their talent acknowledged in a post-colonial world, artists of non-white descent (including First Nations peoples) have fought a far more difficult battle for recognition.

Janson's design was inspired by the collage work of Afro-American artist Romare Bearden (1914–1988). Bearden was born in North Carolina but lived in New York's Harlem most of his life. He trained in New York and Europe, and his work was influenced by European artists Georges Braque (1881–1963), George Grosz (1893–1959), and Fernand Léger (1881–1955), among others. Bearden was a central figure in the Harlem Renaissance, a cultural movement of the 1920s characterized by manifest pride in Afro-American heritages that resulted in a profuse expressive outpouring of art, music, dance, theatre, and literature. Although Bearden's work itself was not used, Janson felt it important to adapt his collage style to represent images of important people and events from Afro-American history on the set of *Harlem Duet.* His influence can be seen in Jansen's costume sketches and in two collages that were mounted on the walls of the set. (Coincidentally, Janson also designed a production of *Othello* in 1987 starring Howard Rollins (1950–1996), the first non-white actor to perform this role at the Stratford Festival.)

THE POSSIBLE WORLDS EXHIBITION offers a rare public forum for the public presentation of work by contemporary Canadian theatre artists. As a relatively new field of study, theatre designs are rarely seen outside of archival collections. Canadian theatre practitioners engage, produce, reinterpret, and adapt the work of Shakespeare, in the pursuit of personal, regional, and national identities. In the context of Shakespeare—Made in Canada, the adaptive nature of design practice illuminates the seminal role of theatre artists in the adaptation and (re)invention of Shakespearean productions in a multicultural Canadian context. In this exhibition, the renderings, set models, and storyboards by Canadian theatre designers are works of art, skilfully rendered, stylistically rich, and distinct.

ENDNOTES

1   Pat Flood, interview with the artist, July 2006.

2   Pat Flood, e-mail correspondence with the artist, September 2006.

3   Pat Flood, e-mail correspondence with the artist, August 2006.

Pat Flood is a theatre, film, and television designer and assistant professor in the School of English and Theatre Studies at the University of Guelph. She has designed for theatres across Canada, including the Stratford Festival for seven seasons. Her most recent work has been as the set designer for Atom Egoyan's film *Where the Truth Lies.* Her television credits include art direction for *La Femme Nikita* and *The Kids in the Hall.*

girlswørk

At the core of *girlswørk*

AT THE CORE of *girlswørk* is the work that women do to make their stories and voices heard by surfacing the ideological structures, among others, messaged through Shakespeare, that continue to efface and (re)shape historic and present-day conditions.

girlswørk is an adaptation of William Shakespeare's *Romeo and Juliet* and, in its meta-theatrics and adaptation-processes, the play examines the coupling of Shakespeare (British literature) with the writers of contemporary capitalism (Canadian advertising), a gesture that questions how literary production (as media) is a transaction of power, a power that continues to fortify a patriarchal hierarchy that determines place based on gender, race, class, and sexuality. *girlswørk* voices how the diverse cultures and histories in solitary lives are bound by and sown from a similar colonial and literary seed—Shakespeare. It is not until the architecture of the literary framework becomes visible that it can be confronted, dismantled, and turned to ash.

For the play's characters, the past informing the present and the present informing the past culminates with the *Shakespeare Women* gathering to become mobile and active agents by disrobing from the garments that bind them.

The images that accompany the following excerpt from *girlswørk* are part of the multimedia projections used during the play's performance.

girlswørk   *an excerpt*

ROSALINE: "Mijn naam is Tryn, Tryn the Cupping
Woman," I kept telling them as they tied me to the
pole, //

JULIET: I liked Smouch's window. She turned her back to
me and //

ROSALINE: as they tore my mother away. Jannetje
Hendricx, her name coarsely etched, with a needle and
black thread, into the palm of my hand. See these? Scars
like veins. //

JULIET: I could see her ass as I threw down seeds to the
Dam Square pidgins. Why should I have been there? Me,
of all people. But I was there. I put my hand on her glass.
She hated that. She hated what she saw in my eyes. //

ROSALINE: When I was small, my father combed my hair
at night. I don't know why he stopped? He'd hum and
comb my hair and then he stopped. //

JULIET: Do you know that in Friesland they were
shocked by women who embraced in public, counted
family coins, skated with torches, feasted through the
night at taverns and ale houses while the city gates
locked? //

ROSALINE: In the Spinhuis, I spun their thread until my shoulder blades bled. They carved the words into my back. A monument of Fallen. Flogging me. Look! Branding me. Juliet. (*Louder*) Juliet, tell me, how do I turn my sewing needle into a navigator? They told me, I had fallen. I kept telling them ... //

JULIET: Here's to skating and torches. (*Lifts glass*)

ROSALINE: I kept telling them ... //

LADY CAPULET: What did you tell them?

ROSALINE: (ROSALINE *looks up.*) That I was pushed.

LADY CAPULET: Nurse, why so quiet? Let's have a toast: To the campaign. To the real authors!

JULIET: Where's the Apothecary?

NURSE: Here's to those who write about us, yet know nothing.

LADY CAPULET: It's not about us, dear. We're just being used to sell their ideas.

NURSE: And that's not a problem because ...?

ROSALINE: Hoeveel kost je per nacht?

JULIET: Here's to Sycorax. (*Raises her glass*)

ALL: To Sycorax!

ROSALINE: We should've invited her.

NURSE: She was invited. We're all invited.

ROSALINE: Are we?

NURSE: She's still digging her way out.

JULIET: Here's to Lavinia. (*Raises her glass*)

ALL: To Lavinia!

ROSALINE: Hmmm? (*Putting hand to ear*) No answer from Lavinia. (*Some laughter*)

JULIET: (*Dead serious*) I don't find that funny at all.

NURSE: *A pattern, precedent and lively warrant. A pattern, prec … //*

LADY CAPULET: (*Interrupting*) Now girls, this has become far too serious. Rosaline, pass the wine and Nurse tell the story about the Queen's priest. //

NURSE: *… edent.* I've grown tired of that story. Rosaline. (*Louder*) Rosaline! Did you know that the word *boss* is Dutch? Means master.

LADY CAPULET: Humour me.

ROSALINE: I thought it was Romanian for *round knob.*

LADY CAPULET: Both apply.

(*The women laugh, pour more wine.*)

NURSE: I've another story. One about a girl who gathered broken shells from the North Sea; //

JULIET: I've been to the sea, but the water //

NURSE: she was happiest there, and she'd watch her brother and his friends swim until they were sky blue. //

JULIET: cut me and the noise //

NURSE: They'd chase me until I couldn't breathe, my pockets full of mute shells, //

JULIET: burned my hand.

NURSE: slowed me, felled me //

ROSALINE: All our shores touch. Plates we can eat from. Did you ever think of that?

NURSE: slathering like dogs. I could hear their feet as they dragged me over the hardened sand.

LADY CAPULET: Oh, please, just tell me the story of the Queen's priest. Wait, do you hear the ceiling rattle? What is that banging?

JULIET: Ophelia's power is in her madness, //

ROSALINE: Then Dr. Charcot posed her, gagged her, undressed her in the mouth of medicine, prescribing the swallowing of supplication.

JULIET: in her voice. She had to die. Like me, like us.

NURSE: A Father of neurology and a Father of literature. //

ROSALINE: Turned her into an owl. You know Ophelia's mad-songs, don't you? Taking //

NURSE: Bad combo, and //

ROSALINE: the bread, the baker's daughter wouldn't give to //

NURSE: enough to drive us mad. //

ROSALINE: Christ.

NURSE: *Lord, we know what we are.*

JULIET: I want to hear Augustine's voice. Ask her where Charcot scarred her, //

ROSALINE: Don't you see! They stole our bread.

LADY CAPULET: Because she's dangerous, disobedient, all of them, all of us.

JULIET: blaming her womb as he opened her thighs.

ROSALINE: Dr. Charcot Hysteria Show. His Ophelias, his Lady Macbeths. Hear them get unruly.

ALL: girlswork

LADY CAPULET: Ohhh, humour me. Please. Hands to ears! Stop banging cursed walls.

JULIET: I can hear them.

NURSE: (NURSE *looks at* LADY CAPULET *and touches her hand.*) The Queen's priest wore a dirty diamond in his navel and a flaming Jezebel, tattooed, on his butt.

(*They all laugh and pass the meat and pudding. Doorbell. A message arrives.*)

NURSE: It's from the Apothecary. It says: "Don't want to play any more."

JULIET: (*Runs to the door. Takes the piece of paper.*) Rosetta! My Romeo.

LADY CAPULET: Do you know what it's called when men get old and they hit the wall with their cane? //

JULIET: I like the way of her tongue, dipping, a loose taste, burning like glass //

LADY CAPULET: girlswork

JULIET: sand

NURSE: These costumes are so heavy //

JULIET: Mother, why are we here?

NURSE: so heavy.

LADY CAPULET: (*Looking up at the ceiling, across the walls; she smoothes down her costume with her hands.*) To make them smell good.

NURSE: Liar.

SOROUJA MOLL

On adaptation and *girlswørk*

> JULIET (*energetically*) I'm not a slave just so they can pierce
> my breasts with scented punches, nor an oracle for those
> trembling with love at the edge of the cities. My whole
> dream had to do with the smell of the fig tree and the
> waist of the one who cuts the shoots of wheat. Nobody
> through me! I through all of you!
> — Federico Garcia Lorca, from *El público* (*The Public*), an
> adaptation of *Romeo and Juliet* and *A Midsummer Night's
> Dream*

ADAPTATION IS PROCESS. Process is change and Lorca, like Lorca does,
changes the way wheat shoots, waists bend, love *trembles.* For me, Lorca
changed Shakespeare by *changing* Shakespeare. Shakespeare can be
changed!

unbound undone undressed untexted understood other ways

Adaptation is disobedient. A cheeky beast. And more than anything,
girlswork is unruly, kicking cans against the stone walls of literary history—making some dents, some noise, some change.

As an adaptation of *Romeo and Juliet,* the work of *girlswørk* is to resist
the pattern and precedent of Shakespeare's play by resurfacing, in other
ways, the oppressive domination of Capulet over his daughter Juliet.
girlswørk sets out to denaturalize Shakespeare's patriarchal template, the
superstructure that positioned—and continues to position—women
and men in specific roles and to assigned places. Reconstructed and
reinforced during Britain's early modern period, these roles have been
manoeuvred and manipulated through history into the architecture of
present-day Canadian theatrical / economic / social situations.

Adaptation can both destroy again and heal again.

Adaptation is blasphemous. Released from good behaviour, girlswork takes the literary god's name in vain, happily defaming, reproach-
ing, destabilizing embedded associations and relationships made nor-
mative, universal. Adaptation asks the painful questions, questions that

93

make mouths go dry, questions asked without asking but asking as directly as can be asked—without blinking. Adaptation is a beating heart. A living body

inhaling exhaling inhaling exhaling inhaling

Adaptation is meta-theatre. A process of examining itself and how Shakespeare's language, devices, directions, and tropes are organized and continue to be used to (re)shape who we are, how we stand next to each other on the bus, how our mouths touch, and how we fight with swords. The protagonists in *girlswørk* are bound to their present desires that are implicitly and explicitly linked to the past, a literary historic past they carry and manifest in how they live, work, love, and die with and without each other. *girlswørk* is about father and daughter, patriarchy and coffeemakers, boys and girls, skating and Dr. Charcot, madness and photocopiers, girls and girls, ad guys and buried bibles, chainsaws and bad ideas, stealing and Ophelia, Christ and daggers, Juliet and torches.

The process of *girlswørk* is not done and probably never will be as it continues to scrutinize Shakespearean frameworks, as well as its (re)configured ideologies, by activating agents to resist, to question, to change, to turn things to ash.

Unabashed, adaptation vandalizes (and doesn't even think about running away). It can be a literary intervention that breaks the tight-lipped nodding rhythm demanded by sacred institutions. girlswork opens mouths and tombs, frightening the purists because they know, deep down, they will never, ever see Juliet the same way again: "Nobody through me! I through all of you!" Once changed, adaptation alters what is written in stone, and turns it into loose sand, tenacious voices, new meanings.

Adaptation is what we know—with a surprise. Tradition tidies up. Adaptation spills the milk. Turbulently. Quietly. Never soft. Always vocal. Sometimes silent. History must never ever be static. With *girlswørk,* I gladly drop the artifact to the floor and begin to chip away at the immoveable Shakespearean granite until I can hold it in the palm of my hand. Look at each piece, each word, see how they collide, *hear how they tremble at the edge of the cities. girlswørk* is an adaptation-in-process (in change) that flexes imperfectly against the canon's skin, punctures its boundaries, clumsily breaks through, and comes out telling the work of girls that's always been done, spoken, and then effaced. Girls' work on the frontiers, the liminal spaces, the hands-on-hips-spaces—making strides without mincing oaths.

> Shakespeare is dangerous—in its beauty. If I listen close,
> it says "**language is power**,"
>
> and Adaptation says back, "**here, have some**."

I AM GRATEFUL to Daniel Fischlin, my faculty advisor at the University of Guelph, for supporting and encouraging my play writing (and its mischievous tangents). Through the processes of adaptation, I turned a three-page assignment into a forty-two-page play that questions the multiple ways Shakespeare's early modern literary relationship is ever-present in contemporary social situations.

My immeasurable thanks to Dawn Owen—for her girlswork.

Sorouja Moll is a Guelph, Ontario, writer. Her work has been on CBC Radio and published in the *Globe and Mail*, *Toronto Star*, *Carousel Literary Journal*, and *Today's Parent*. Moll's academic publications include her research writing for the Canadian Adaptations of Shakespeare Project (CASP) website at the University of Guelph. Currently, she is co-creating and co-producing a short video documentary concerning Aboriginal Shakespearean adaptations in Canada. In 2003, she received first prize in the Eden Mills Writers' Festival Literary Contest. Moll has also participated in spoken word performances at the Hillside Festival, Eden Mills Writers' Festival, and other regional events.

LEANORE LIEBLEIN

Pourquoi Shakespeare?

Why Shakespeare?

THIS WAS THE QUESTION posed by Jean Gascon, founding co-director of Montreal's Théâtre du Nouveau Monde (TMN) and director of the Stratford Festival 1968–74, to his audience in 1962 when the TNM mounted its first play by Shakespeare. Gascon answered by describing the staging of *Richard II* as a rendezvous with destiny: "Because we have dreamed of this meeting with the most important dramatic poet for a long time. He has become necessary to us." For Gascon, Shakespeare was "such a dramatic genius that his singular voice traverses the barrier of language and reaches us with incredible force." But Gascon also felt it was necessary to "jostle" [*bousculer*] Shakespeare: "Without wanting to take liberties with the author, we have wanted to feel ourselves free." The protection of one's own freedom in the face of Shakespeare's apparent hugeness has been a persistent feature of French Canada's encounter with the Bard.

Though there were occasional productions of Shakespeare in French—in December 1923, the Odéon theatre company of Paris presented four plays in French, two of them by Shakespeare—it was largely in English that Shakespeare, brought by British and American touring companies, came to French Canada in the nineteenth century. Indeed Jean Béraud,

LEFT Production photograph from *La Nuit des Rois* (Théâtre du Nouveau Monde, 2002)

in his *350 ans de théâtre au Canada français* [*350 Years of Theatre in French Canada*], cites numerous English language productions of Shakespeare precisely because they were attended by francophones. But the combination of the lure of Shakespeare and the desire for cultural independence expressed by Jean Gascon in 1962 had been present in French Canada since at least the early 1830s. As Leonard Doucette has described in his history of theatre in French Canada, that was when the "Amateurs Canadiens" and the "Amateurs de Montréal," seeking an alternative to the vaudeville, melodrama, and farce brought by French touring companies, combined to perform *Hamlet* and *Othello* in the adaptations of the French Ducis. Thus 175 years ago, Shakespeare was used in French Canada, along with Molière, Scribe, and others to assert local taste and resist the superficiality of imported culture.

Passing the Shakespeare Test

TWO PHENOMENA IN the 1930s and 1940s contributed to the conspicuous emergence of a Shakespearean presence in French Canada at a time when theatre was suffering from the after-effects of the First World War, the Spanish flu, and the Great Depression, as well as from the competition offered by cinema and commercially motivated popular theatre. The first was the important contribution of the new media of radio and television. Taking seriously its mandate of enriching the cultural life of the people, Radio-Canada and other stations presented versions of "masterpieces of world theatre." According to Madeleine Greffard in an overview of radio theatre in French Canada from its beginnings to the advent of television, these included *Othello* and *Hamlet* on CHLP (Montreal) in 1938–1939, *Othello* on Radio-Canada in 1940, and in 1945–1946 and 1947–1948 *Macbeth, Hamlet, Roméo et Juliette,* and *Othello* on Radio-Collège of Radio-Canada. Similarly, Télétheâtre of Radio-Canada broadcast *La mégère apprivoisée* [*The Taming of the Shrew*] in 1953, and *Roméo et Juliette* in 1958.

In the same period, the appearance of new theatre companies and playwrights contributed to the beginnings of an impressive professional theatre milieu in which Shakespeare found a home. Among the companies seeking alternatives to a theatrical diet of burlesque and revues was L'Équipe, founded by the nineteen-year-old Pierre Dagenais in 1942. His

Songe d'une nuit d'été [*A Midsummer Night's Dream*], produced outdoors in the gardens of the Ermitage, was, by all accounts, magical. Similarly, the Compagnons de Saint-Laurent, founded in 1937 by Father Émile Legault, produced an unforgettable *Soir des rois* [*Twelfth Night*] in 1946.

Production photograph from *Roméo et Juliette* (Radio Canada, 1958)

The Compagnons's production illustrates the audacity and complexity of the Québécois relation to Shakespeare. On one hand, the mise en scène of Père Legault, who had spent time in France, showed the influence of important productions of *Twelfth Night* by Harley Granville-Barker at the Savoy in London in 1912 and Jacques Copeau in the opening season of the Vieux Colombier in Paris in 1914. But though the presence of European modernism was unmistakable, it was transformed by the contribution of internationally known Québec artist Alfred Pellan. Pellan's set and costume designs for the Compagnons's *Soir des rois* showed the inventiveness and originality of a great artist untrammelled by preconceptions of what constituted a Shakespearean aesthetic. They may have been executed on a miniscule budget, with their fantastic detail hand-painted on cloth backdrops that sagged when unrolled, but to the critics the experience was of one great artist meeting another. In 1967, Jean-Louis Roux, preparing a Québec contribution to the tenth anniversary celebrations of the Stratford Festival in Ontario, came across Pellan's designs and was enchanted. He consequently

99

Production photograph from
Richard II (Théâtre du Nouveau
Monde, 1962)

used the designs a second time in his 1968 production for the Théâtre du Nouveau Monde. The music for Roux's production was by Gabriel Charpentier, who has composed music for numerous Shakespeare productions at the TNM and the Stratford Festival. Charpentier's musical creations for the theatre start with a visually striking graphic analysis of each play.

It is the costumes of Orsino and Olivia as recreated in the 1968 *Nuit des rois* that appear in the Shakespeare—Made in Canada exhibition. In them, we see Pellan's playfulness, the brilliance of his palette, and his evocation of the *commedia dell'arte.* Orsino's costume, with its skirted doublet, diagonal stripes, and windowpane checks, combines a sixteenth-century profile with modernist motifs. Decorative elements on the costumes contribute to a reading of the characters. For example, Olivia's black-veiled headdress, topped by a coffin decorated with crosses, teardrops, and a heart, suggests both a catafalque and a bed, and is a sign of her love for her dead brother; and her pearls (like those of Elizabeth I) are an emblem of her chastity. But, along with the elegance and elaborateness of her dress, the headpiece also suggests her self-indulgence and narcissism.

The first works of Shakespeare to be performed in this period were largely among the most popular and accessible of Shakespeare's plays. Between 1945 and 1969, Gilbert David's theatrography includes *A Midsummer Night's Dream* (1945, 1965), *Twelfth Night* (1946, 1956, 1968), *Romeo and Juliet* (1950), *The Taming of the Shrew* (1956, 1966), *Richard II* (1962), and *The Merchant of Venice* (1963). Photographs of these and other productions from the private collection of Charles Bolster are included in the Shakespeare—Made in Canada exhibition. It is interesting, however, that when the Théâtre du Nouveau Monde, founded in 1951 and committed to performing the *grand répertoire,* entered the Shakespeare fray in 1962, the play they chose to tackle was not a romantic comedy. It was by taking on the challenge of staging *Richard II,* a play at the centre of English national history, that they chose to demonstrate their ability to "pass the Shakespeare test."

Shakespeare, Prince of Québec

THE PERIOD OF THE 1960S in Québec is known as the *Révolution tranquille* [Quiet Revolution]. It followed nearly twenty years of government under Québec Premier Maurice Duplessis—years that were marked by a commitment to conservative ideology, traditional values, and resistance to change, accompanied by a secularization of the society and a decline in the birth rate. The election of Premier Jean Lesage (1960–1966) initiated a process of reform that included such things as democratization of the system of education, revision of the labour code, and nationalization of Hydro-Québec. The 1960s also saw, in conjunction with movements of national liberation worldwide, the creation of a movement for the independence of Québec from the rest of Canada. By 1967, the centenary of Canadian Confederation and the year of Expo 67, the movement had found its stride. A landmark moment was the visit to Québec of French Prime Minister Charles de Gaulle whose words "Vive le Québec libre" [Long live a free Québec] resounded from the balcony of Montreal's City Hall. The "nouveau théâtre québécois" [new Québec theatre], as it was called by Michel Bélair in a 1973 book of that title, was one site of cultural affirmation. In the words of playwright Claude Levac, "When Québec playwrights will have found an armature, a theatrical structure that is our very own and the equal of our collective dorsal spine, we will not only have found an authentic dramaturgy which is our own, but also a country." And there, in a series of adaptations participating in this impulse towards cultural self-realization, was Shakespeare.

Hamlet, prince du Québec by Robert Gurik (1968) couldn't have been more explicit. It was a political allegory that used Shakespeare's *Hamlet* to explore the complexities and ambiguities of Québec in Canada. Hamlet, of course, was Québec. He and the Gravediggers, representative of two generations of the Québec people, were the only characters who did not wear masks. King Claudius was L'Anglophonie, the English-speaking world of economic and political control, and Queen Gertrude was his partner in power, l'Église [the Church]. Polonius was Prime Minister Lester B. Pearson; his daughter Ophélie, Québec Premier

Production photograph from
Hamlet, prince du Québec
(Théâtre de L'Escale, 1968)

Jean Lesage; and his son Laerte, Prime Minister-in-Waiting Pierre Elliott Trudeau. Hamlet's friend Horatio, prophetically, was René Lévesque. The Ghost of Hamlet's father was Charles de Gaulle. And so it went. The equivalents were spelled out in the program, the published text, and on masks in the form of political caricatures. The exhibition includes four of the costume designs by Renée Noiseux-Gurik and four of the masks by Guy Monarque, and a spear used at the end of the play, as well as production photos.

Gurik's play was only a beginning. In 1970, Jean-Claude Germain's musical *Rodéo et Juliette,* drawing on the annual "Festival Western" of the Québec village of Saint Tite, created a new version of Shakespeare's love story. His Juliette could only love a man who would follow his dream of creating a different world. In 1977, Jean-Pierre Ronfard, whose love affair with Shakespeare would be carried out in many plays throughout his life, created a travestied Lear whose debased kingdom was a pizza, whose throne was a case of Coca Cola, and whose elder daughters were obsessed with money and sex.

And so: "Why Shakespeare?" Why use the iconic poet of British cultural authority to contest that culture and its authority? Part of the answer is suggested by the presence in Gurik's play of Charles de Gaulle as the paternal ghost. In the 1970s, the French heritage of Québec was experienced as an ambiguous legacy. After the defeat of Montcalm on the Plains of Abraham in 1759, the French were felt by many to have abandoned the *habitants* to Britain. Nevertheless, to the denigration of

Québécois language and culture, French language and culture continued to haunt Québec as a model of desirability and correctness. To use Shakespeare was to turn one's back on the likes of Corneille, Racine, and Molière. To use Shakespeare against the English—to make his work serve one's own nationalist and cultural ends—was to assert one's freedom to do so. The immense liberty with which Shakespeare is both celebrated and defaced in these adaptations makes Shakespeare a partner in the project of an independent Québec.

Production photograph from *King Lear* (Nouveau Théâtre Experimental, 1977)

Shakespeare and the Québec Language

IT WAS IN THIS CONTEXT that Michel Garneau translated *Macbeth de William Shakespeare* into Québécois. Before 1968, when Jean-Louis Roux did his own French translation for the production of *Twelfth Night* he was about to direct, translations of Shakespeare performed in Québec had been made in France. Ten years later in 1978, two years before the referendum on Québec sovereignty, Garneau's translation asserted that Québécois was not a dialect, not a *jargon*, but a language. And language was at the heart of Québécois cultural and national identity.

Based on French as it was still spoken in the Gaspé peninsula of Québec, Garneau's Québécois was closer to the seventeenth-century French spoken in France in Shakespeare's day than to modern French. Garneau brought *Macbeth* closer to his audience by eliminating reminders of its foreignness. As Annie Brisset has pointed out in her study of

103

theatrical translation in Québec, the drums of "A drum, a drum! / Macbeth doth come" became the *violons* of French Canadian fiddle music; wood and heath became the *forêt* and *brûlé* of the Québec landscape; and Scotland became *"not' pauv' pays,"* our poor country in need of liberation from a tyrannical oppressor. Garneau subsequently translated two other plays by Shakespeare, *The Tempest* in 1982 and *Coriolanus* in 1989. In 1993, internationally known theatre artist Robert Lepage created a *Cycle Shakespeare* for the National Arts Centre in Ottawa, for the Festival de Théâtre des Amériques in Montreal, and for a world tour: a production of all three Garneau translations to represent three genres, three production styles, and "a journey into the evolution of a language." A video expressly created for the Shakespeare—Made in Canada exhibition, with excerpts from these three productions, illustrates the relationship among the dramatic texts, their language, and their mise en scène.

Shakespearean Spring

THE SHAKESPEAREAN PRESENCE in the 1980s contributed to the expansiveness and self-confidence of the Québec theatrical institution with, at one end, Jean-Pierre Ronfard's monumental six-part *Vie et mort du roi boiteux* [*Life and Death of the Limping King*] in 1981, and at the other, *Printemps Shakespeare* [*Shakespearean Spring*] of 1988. With the question of political independence for the moment laid to rest by the referendum of 1980, Québec theatre artists revelled in the capacity of theatre to create worlds and to cross boundaries. Ronfard's fanciful epic of rival clans depicted a fictional world that ranged from Abitibi to Azerbaijan and left no continent untouched. His limping king was at once both Shakespeare's Richard III and King Lear, but also Oedipus, Hamlet, Orestes, and others.

The spring of 1988 saw major productions in Montreal of no fewer than six of Shakespeare's plays: *A Midsummer Night's Dream* directed by Robert Lepage at the Théâtre du Nouveau Monde; *The Tempest* directed by Alice Ronfard at the Espace Go; and *Richard II, Henry IV* (Parts One and Two), and *Henry V* as the *Cycle des rois* [*Kings' Cycle*] directed by Jean Asselin of Théâtre Omnibus at the Espace Libre. Their splendour and variety is seen in the slide sequence in the exhibition in which one can see the spiralling phallic forest of *Songe d'une nuit d'été,* the massive video screens dominating the square of sand that represented Prospero's island in *La tempête,* and the impossibly steep steps that formed the backdrop to the acrobatic movements of actors in the *Cycle des rois.*

The costumes and props on display in the exhibition give some idea of the contrasting aesthetics of these productions. With the oversized curves and angles of its silhouette, its spiralled breasts, and the layered richness of its fabrics, Meredith Caron's costume for an imperious and disdainful Titania is a hyperreal rendition of a baroque aesthetic. Her costume for Bottom the weaver—a beautiful and witty combination of rich velvet in Elizabethan profile held together by numerous long and heavy metallic zippers—masterfully expresses Bottom as both a "mechanical" and a man of unlimited imagination. In contrast to the scenic lushness of *Songe* is the stripped-down aesthetic of the *Cycle des Rois* by Yvan Gaudin, whose costume for Falstaff is also seen in the exhibition. His award-winning costumes for 135 characters performed by fourteen actors were created by raiding the second-hand shops of the east end of Montreal—much like furs for Charlotte Dean's costumes for a 1995 production of *King Lear* came from Toronto thrift shops. In Gaudin's *Cycle des Rois,* a bird cage became the French king's crown; a film reel, a bishop's mitre; a crutch and length of lead pipe, as seen in the exhibition, a harquebus.

All of these productions celebrated their theatricality and invited spectators to do the same. Puck became an agent of theatrical transformation as (s)he rotated the platform of *Le Songe.* In *La Tempête,* Prospero was played by the actress Françoise Faucher and was occasionally accompanied by an additional character called "The Actor." The choreographed movements of actors in the *Cycle des rois* were multiplied by reflecting side panels in which spectators also saw themselves as an audience.

Whose Shakespeare?

IN 1996, THE FIVE-EVENING EVENT called *38* implicitly challenged such big budget Shakespeare(s) and questioned the ownership of Shakespeare by generously subsidized companies. Instead, it explored an alternative to expensive productions with large casts that left few crumbs of opportunity for young playwrights. Thirty-eight authors under the age of thirty-eight were invited to write and direct fifteen-minute monologues, each based on a different work by Shakespeare.

Production poster for *38*
(Théâtre Urbi and Orbi and
Théâtre d'aujourd'hui, 1996)

Deploying the immensely popular Québécois form of the *conte urbain* [urban tale] against a colourful backdrop of Shakespearean graffiti, the event used the authority of Shakespeare to display the creativity, multiplicity, and variety of new Québec playwriting, and to give stage time to those for whom it was largely inaccessible. In an impressive celebration of youthful talent, *38* staged an encounter with Shakespeare that was variously playful, respectful, satiric, resentful, sardonic, and humorous.

38 merely confirmed the multiplicity of subject positions from which Shakespeare has persistently been addressed in French Canada. In the case of the explicitly political adaptations of the 1960s and 1970s, we have already seen Shakespeare used to further the political aspirations of Québec. Numerous subsequent adaptations have continued to address Shakespeare with other agendas and points of view. In 1980, for example, Jacques Girard and Reynald Robinson created *Roméo et Julien*, a delightful cabaret-style two-hander that explored in personal terms issues of gender and sexuality. By contrast, Tibor Egervari, writing out of his experience as a man of the theatre and a Shoah survivor, wrote *Le Marchand de Venise de Shakespeare à Auschwitz* [*Shakespeare's The Merchant of Venice in Auschwitz*] (1977; rev. 1998) in which he imagined a concentration camp commander directing Jewish, homosexual, and gypsy prisoners in a performance in which he himself played a deliberately anti-Semitic role of Shylock.

Since the 1990s, received readings of Shakespeare, in particular, have been revisited in French Canada. Acadian author Antonine Maillet's *William S* (1991) had Shakespeare's characters questioning the fates he had dealt them, and in *Sauvée des eaux* [*Saved from the Waters*] (2001), Daphné Thompson tried to save Ophelia from drowning. *Hamlet-le-Malécite* [*Hamlet the Malecite*] (2004) by Yves Sioui Durand and Jean-Frédéric Messier created a First Nations Hamlet; *Sous l'empire de Iago* [*Subject to the Empire of Iago*] by Kadar Mansour (2002) offered a postcolonial *Othello*; and *Dave veut jouer Richard III* [*Dave Wants to Play Richard III*] by Alexis Martin (2001) explored the desire of a handicapped actor to perform Shakespeare's deformed king. Even Michel Garneau's politicized 1978 translation of *Macbeth* into Québécois was resituated into a longer his-

torical context by Robert Lepage in 1993 as can be seen in the video mentioned earlier.

While Shakespeare in French Canada continues to be rich, the definition of French Canada has continued to change. In the play *Le Making of de Macbeth* (1996) by Jean-Frédéric Messier (based on an original idea by Paula de Vasconcelos), the artistically creative act of producing a play is juxtaposed with the biologically creative act of having a child; social classes, languages, and ethnicities bump up against one another.

Production photograph from *Le Marchand de Venise de Shakespeare à Auschwitz* (Théâtre Distinct, Université D'Ottawa, 1977)

Shakespeare Ongoing

SHAKESPEAREAN ADAPTATIONS are, etymologically speaking, "eccentric"—out (outside) of the "centre" of what is, conventionally, taken to be "Shakespeare." In addition to the fascinating proliferation of Shakespearean adaptations in French, two phenomena suggest the persistent presence of francophone Shakespeare at its centre, as well as on its margins.

In 1939, Maurice Lebel, former dean of the Faculté des Lettres of Laval University, made clear in his *Suggestions pratiques sur notre enseigne-*

 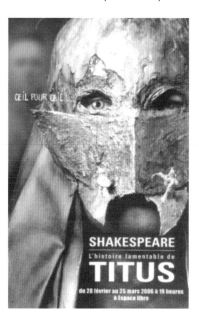

Production poster for *Sauvée des eaux* (Théâtre de l'Esquisse, 2000)

Production poster for *L'histoire lamentable de Titus* (Omnibus at l'Espace Libre, 2006)

ment that Shakespeare, at least at the secondary school level, could not be a priority: "Should one study a play by Shakespeare? I don't think so. How can one expect students to get something out of studying Shakespeare when, in most of our secondary schools [collèges], teachers don't even explain a tragedy by Corneille or by Racine, a comedy by Beaumarchais, or a drama by Victor Hugo? For myself, I would never risk putting even a single one of [Shakespeare's] plays on the syllabus." Nevertheless, Les Compagnons de Saint-Laurent, the first professional theatre company in Québec, grew out of the collaboration of a group of classical college students with their teacher; it went on to produce *Le soir des rois* in 1946 and *Roméo et Juliette* in 1958. Since then, as the magnificent posters on display suggest, Shakespeare certainly has been present in the work of young performers.

The theatrography of such established companies as the Théâtre du Rideau Vert in Montreal and the Théâtre du Trident at the Grand Théâtre in Québec indicates a number of Shakespeare productions over the years. Most astonishing, as seen in this exhibition, the Théâtre du Nouveau Monde has produced no fewer than twenty productions of Shakespeare since 1968. In addition, a glance at the recently completed 2005–2006 season, reveals in Montreal a musical version of *Antony and Cleopatra* at the TNM and a production of *L'Histoire lamentable de Titus* [*The Lamentable Story of Titus*] by Omnibus at L'Espace Libre. There were also two adaptations in Québec City: *Les mots fantômes [Phantom Words],* an adaptation of *Hamlet* by Michel Nadeau created by the Théâtre Niveau Parking; and *Autour du Boiteux [On the Subject of the Boiteux],* a reflection on *King Lear* by Pascal Lafond for the Théâtre des Fonds de Tiroirs, which grew out of their earlier celebrated work on Ronfard's *Vie et mort du roi Boiteux.* This sense of a persistent francophone Shakespearean presence is confirmed by the Canadian Adaptations of Shakespeare Project. Of the numerous adaptations of Shakespeare since pre-Confederation identified on its website, about one quarter derive from French Canada.

Le grand Will

THE FRANCOPHONE RELATIONSHIP to Shakespeare is perhaps best expressed in the phrase frequently used to refer to him. Shakespeare is *le grand Will.* He is great, but cut down to size. He is an object of admiration, yet an intimate to whom one can refer by his first name. He is someone with whom one can do battle and still remain friends. He is a stranger who has taken up residence in French Canada and who has changed his hosts as they have changed him.

Former McGill University associate professor and chair of English, and current member of the McGill Shakespeare and Performance Research Team, Leanore Lieblein was recently a visiting professor at the Institut d'Etudes Théâtrales (Université de Paris III—Sorbonne Nouvelle). She has published articles on early modern theatre, theatre archives, theatre criticism, and theatrical translation, and has written extensively on French language responses to Shakespeare. She has also directed medieval, Renaissance, and modern plays.

| YVETTE NOLAN

Julius Caesar:
Adapted to *Death*

I AM NOT SURE when I developed an interest in adapting Shakespeare, or why. In the mid-90s, I did a four-person, cross-gendered, ten-minute *Othello* as part of the Testing Ground series put on by the Popular Theatre Alliance of Manitoba. A couple of years later, I wrote (with Philip Adams) *Shakedown Shakespeare,* a piece of theatre for young audiences that incorporates four of Shakespeare's stories: *Romeo and Juliet, Hamlet, King Lear,* and *Macbeth.* The idea of *Shakedown Shakespeare* is that it serves as a primer; the characters begin the play speaking colloquially, and as the play progresses, more and more of Shakespeare's text is incorporated. Students acquire the language painlessly, incidentally, while their attention is focused elsewhere: on plot, on comedy, on action, on journey. The language does not get in the way; the language is the way, as the adage goes.

I arrived at the adaptation of *Julius Caesar* through the back door. When I took over the artistic direction of Native Earth Performing Arts in 2002, I frequently found myself sitting on panels discussing diversity in theatre. In Toronto, although fully half of the population is not white, theatres were—and still are—struggling to reflect that reality. Ergo, a series of panels on cultural diversity were created. At one such

LEFT Actors Ryan Cunningham, Sara Sinclair, Falen Johnson, Craig Lauzon, Tara Beagan, Cheri Maracle-Cardinal, and Jani Lauzon in *Death of a Chief,* performed at the Festival of Original Theatre (University of Toronto)

event, I glibly remarked, "Why can't Native Earth produce an Aboriginal *Julius Caesar*? It's really just about band politics after all." The idea had sprung from my head and began to nag me.

At about the same time, an actress came to me with a suggestion: why not access some professional development funds and offer a Shakespeare intensive for female Native performers? Native performers are rarely considered for roles in Shakespeare, in part because white producers cannot imagine a Native Desdemona, a Native Lear, unless it is stunt casting. Many of the established Native theatre artists did not come through formal schools or conservatories, and therefore have acquired the tools to work with Shakespeare through a piecemeal process, often finding themselves at a disadvantage when they do audition. I thought a professional development workshop in Shakespeare might at least level the playing field a bit.

Kennedy (Cathy) MacKinnon has a reputation as a teacher of Shakespeare and as a vocal coach. Like me, she loves the language; like me, she believes that his stories have resonance with almost everyone. She has coached at Stratford Festival, taught at the Centre for Indigenous Theatre, and worked with a group in Mozambique to adapt *A Midsummer Night's Dream* to tell their own story. She also runs an annual Shakespeare intensive out of Humber College.

Her work with my small group of Native actors lit a fire in them, and in us. Now that they had the tools, we should capitalize on the knowledge. I confessed my Caesar fantasy, and we began to plot.

We snuck up on the adaptation. In the first week-long workshop, a company of five women and three men spent much of the time acquiring the tools to read and speak Shakespeare's text. We read the folio three times, changing casting each time. We did some physical work, creating tableaux of critical moments, distilling the story into a short movement and vocal piece. We still had no idea where we were heading with the text.

Much of the second and third weeks of the workshop were spent discussing the parallels between our lives and the story of Caesar. The actors had done personal writing that was inspired by the text, about power, identity, community, leadership. They brought writings and stories of others as well, everything from traditional teachings to Trudeau. At the end of the workshop, we presented the work we had done so far at Native Earth's Weesageechak Festival. Our adaptation at this point ended with the third act, after Caesar's death and the eulogies for him delivered by Antony and Brutus. Because we had played with the chronology of the text, the showing actually ended with Antony's speech: "O pardon me, thou bleeding peece of earth: that I am meeke and gentle with these butchers." [1]

By the time we entered our fourth week of workshop, which was precipitated by an invitation to show at the University of Toronto's Festival of Original Theatre (or FOOT), we had begun to incorporate the actors' personal writings into the text. The themes that popped for us—responsibility to a community, the laws a community holds dear and what happens to those who transgress, the responsibility to be true to oneself—began to shape the adaptation. The company members spent much time in a circle discussing what aspects of the Caesar story resonated with them.

The adaptation of *Julius Caesar* into *Death of a Chief* is by no means complete. The process of the adaptation—because it happens in the studio, with the full involvement of the company—is a long, relatively organic process. We are also adapting as a community, and at the same time, we seem to be creating a community. At the most recent workshop, at the University of Guelph, a company member announced that we felt like an ensemble, like a company, and it felt good.

Death of a Chief enters its final development phase in June 2007, when the company of eight or nine actors, two directors, and a choreographer enter the studio for a three-week creation period in anticipation of a full production next season. We still don't know what story we are telling, what the final shape will be. We still don't even know if any of the fourth and fifth acts will find their way into our text. We will discover the answers in a room, together, as a community.

ENDNOTES

1 William Shakespeare, *The Tragedie of Julius Caesar: Applause First Folio Editions,* ed. Neil Freeman (Milwaukee, Wisconsin: Hal Leonard Corp., 1997), 50, 3.1.255. References are to act, scene, and line.

Yvette Nolan is a playwright, director, and dramaturg. Her plays include BLADE, *Job's Wife, Video,* and *Annie Mae's Movement.* She is currently the artistic director of Native Earth Performing Arts in Toronto.

MARION GRUNER

What Means This Shouting?

When work on this short film began, there were so many (perhaps too many) starting points from which to explore Aboriginal adaptations of Shakespeare. Central to these was the complicated relationship between Canada's Nicholas Flood Davin—nineteenth-century journalist, politician, and architect of the profoundly damaging residential school system—and Shakespearean texts.

Sorouja Moll, the film's co-producer, had written a paper called *The Davin Report: Shakespeare and Canada's Manifest Destiny,* available on the Canadian Adaptations of Shakespeare Project website <www.canadianshake-speares.ca/essays/davin.cfm>. The essay studies Davin and the myriad connections between his work in public policy and the colonial imperative of the time, a directive that not only devastated a culture, but also virtually erased Aboriginal women from Canadian public policy. In painstaking detail, Moll shows the links among Davin,

What Means This Shouting? is a short documentary film, co-produced by Marion Gruner and Sorouja Moll, that explores contemporary Aboriginal adaptations of Shakespeare. Its focus is *Death of a Chief,* an adaptation of *Julius Caesar* in which many of the male character roles are cast as female. *Death of a Chief* is co-adapted and co-directed by Yvette Nolan and Kennedy (Cathy) MacKinnon for Native Earth Performing Arts.

LEFT Film stills from *What Means This Shouting?*

From L to R: (still 1) Clifford Cardinal, Monique Mojica; (still 4) Jani Lauzon, Michaela Washburn; (still 5) Michelle St. John, Michaela Washburn; (still 6) Jani Lauzon, Monique Mojica; and (still 8) Cheri Maracle-Cardinal

115

Shakespeare, and colonization. Her work shines a new light on the current state of Aboriginal women in Canada—particularly the epidemic of disappeared women and the judicial and police inaction that has accompanied it. The paper's conclusion offers a strong female voice: Yvette Nolan, a Toronto playwright and director who uses Shakespearean adaptation to confront present-day Native issues in Canada. Both Sorouja and I kept returning to Nolan's work as the early ideas for the film unfolded.

And then there was the Bard himself—the iconic yet troubling Shakespeare—the jewel of the English literary canon. What did it mean for artists who had been deprived of their own language and culture to take a 400-year-old English text and make it their own? The answer was, of course, as straightforward as any definition of adaptation, since with great love for the Bard, these First Nations artists were turning the canon on its end to explore the realities of their communities in complex ways.

So: a very rich vein to mine and distill into six minutes.

In the end, what spoke most clearly was one concrete, living, and ongoing experience: Yvette Nolan's *Death of a Chief,* a work-in-progress with female directors, female writers, and a predominantly female cast. Using *Julius Caesar* as the source text, Nolan and her actors explore dysfunction in Native governments and the roles their communities play in it. As Nolan says, "We've lost our land, we've lost our language ... I don't know what the answer is. And I guess that's one of the things we're pushing against with *Death of a Chief* ... with such flawed systems, and such pitiful tools, how do we create a new way of going forward? Because what we've picked up—the tools we've got—are picked up from the colonizer, you know? We've lost track of what it was we were doing." From Native Earth Performing Arts' perspective, they are not merely reviving a play by a dead white male, but are also grappling with the story of their people as it is being "played" out now.

Adaptation-in-process is where the most important questions are asked, and it was fascinating to see personal histories meld with political and communal ones to create a truly collaborative work. Moreover, I wanted to know how those creative decisions got made, what informed them, and where the artists found inspiration. At the film's completion,

Death of a Chief remains "in progress," due in part to financial shortfalls that have come about, ironically, because Nolan is consistently questioned by funding agents who wonder about the need for an Aboriginal theatre company to do Shakespeare.

—

THIS FILM IS THE RESULT of many collaborations: co-producer Sorouja Moll has been integral to carrying out the vision; Native Earth Performing Arts opened their process to me; Dawn Matheson and Jennifer Moore of the Pidgeon Collective made for acute guides through difficult and compelling terrain. I thank the Canadian Adaptations of Shakespeare Project for the research impetus and the ongoing support without which this film could not have been made.

Marion Gruner is a producer and multimedia artist who focuses on documentary. She has lived and worked in Guelph since arriving to study English literature at the University of Guelph in 1992.

LORNE BRUCE & LORNA ROURKE

Shakespeare in the L. W. Conolly Theatre Archives

THE UNIVERSITY OF GUELPH LIBRARY'S theatre archives section began in a modest fashion with the acquisition of one small collection in 1969. In the subsequent three-and-half decades, the archival collections have rapidly expanded to form the largest archival theatre holdings in Canada, with a significant portion of those archives devoted to Shakespearean production and adaptation. From the outset, a major collecting focus has been on modern Ontario theatre. Today, in 2007, most major Ontario theatres are represented, as are a number of prominent individual theatre artists who have deposited their own personal records, such as renowned Canadian Shakespearean actor William Hutt. The breadth and depth of Guelph's holdings demonstrate that the work of Canadian playwrights transcends provincial boundaries. Without a doubt, our theatres, performers, playwrights, and designers have had both national and international impact.

The University of Guelph Library's rich and varied collections were named the L. W. Conolly Theatre Archives in 1999 to recognize the leadership of Dr. Leonard Conolly in establishing and sustaining its development while he served as chair of the University's drama department and as vice-president academic in the 1980s and 1990s. The L.W. Conolly Theatre Archives have become a major resource for scholars, not only in Canada but around the world. Naturally, William Shakespeare is well-

LEFT Yorick's skull, production prop from *Hamlet* (Phoenix Theatre, 1981) represented in the theatre archives by entire collections centered on the Bard's plays.

Shakespeare's influence in Canadian, especially Ontarian, drama is most evident in a number of Guelph's major theatre collections. These archival resources form the basis of Guelph's holdings on William Shakespeare. They are available for viewing in Archival and Special Collections in the Wellington County Room, as well as in the library reading room used by students, faculty, researchers, and members of the public. The following collections also include the unique reference code for these materials.

SHAKESPEARE MEMORIAL NATIONAL THEATRE COMMITTEE COLLECTION (UK).

The Committee was established to promote and organize the creation of a National Theatre for Britain. Two "minute books," May 1909–July 1912, are signed on five occasions by Bernard Shaw (1856–1950), and on four occasions by William Archer (1856–1924), the great Scottish theatre critic and translator. Also included is a sheet signed by fifteen members of the Executive Committee. It was not until 1963 that the National Theatre (under Laurence Olivier) opened at the Old Vic in London. [XZ1 MS A106]

WILLIAM HUTT FONDS.

Canada's internationally recognized performer began his professional career in 1948. Hutt joined the Stratford Festival in its first season in 1953 and starred in much of the Shakespeare canon as an actor, director, and associate director until his retirement in 2005. Among the prominent leads he has taken on are Lear, Hamlet, Macbeth, Prospero, Falstaff, Titus, Brutus, Timon, Feste, and Richard II. [XZ1 MS B020, B027]

CANADIAN PLAYERS COLLECTION.

Founded as a national professional touring company for Canada by Tom Patterson and Douglas Campbell, the Canadian Players first toured in 1954, and for the next twelve years took a repertoire of mainly Shakespeare and Shaw across Canada and into the United States. The Canadian Players merged with Crest Theatre in 1966 to form the Crest Players Foundation, which eventually became Theatre Toronto (1968). The collection features programs and reviews, 1955–65. [XZ1 MS A120]

STRATFORD FESTIVAL COLLECTION. Founded in 1953 by Tom Patterson, the Stratford Festival has established itself as one of the world's leading Shakespearean theatre companies. The library holds prompt scripts, programs, posters, articles, publications, promotional materials, press releases, and designs, from 1953 to the present. The collection includes microfilm copies of prompt scripts of all productions, 1953–1970, as well as twenty-nine scrapbooks donated by the London Public Library, Ontario, in 1991. Holdings are selective as the Stratford Festival also maintains its own comprehensive archival collection, recently moved to a new location. Included in the Shakespeare—Made in Canada exhibition is one item of particular interest from Guelph's Stratford holdings, an *As You Like It* costume designed by the celebrated theatre designer Desmond Heeley for a 1959 production. [XZ1 MS A400–414]

BARRY MACGREGOR COLLECTION. Clippings, programs, designs, photographs, and other materials relating to the career of popular actor and director Barry MacGregor, primarily at the Shaw and Stratford Festivals, and the Bastion Theatre (Victoria, BC), 1949 to the present. MacGregor is featured in the Shakespeare—Made in Canada exhibition through production materials for *Henry V* in 1980, *The Merchant of Venice* in 1970, and *The Taming of the Shrew* in 1973. [XZ1 MS A008]

CECIL O'NEAL COLLECTION. Scripts, production files, and administrative records relating to the career of director, administrator, and teacher Cecil O'Neal, particularly relating to his position as director of productions at the Stratford Festival, 1975–1985. [XZ1 MS A121]

ELDA MAGILL CADOGAN COLLECTION. Scrapbooks, clippings, photographs, scripts, correspondence, programs, and financial records, 1937–1994, chiefly relating to Cadogan's play *Rise and Shine* and to Stratford Festival productions. Cadogan was a widely-produced Canadian amateur playwright, particularly in the 1940s and 1950s. [XZ1 MS A148.]

HILARY CORBETT COLLECTION. One of Canada's pre-eminent costume designers, Hilary Corbett moved to Canada from England in 1964 and worked for the Stratford and Shaw Festivals throughout the 1970s. In 1975, she began a twenty-year tenure as a staff designer for CBC Television.

She has designed costumes for major theatre companies across Canada. There are approximately 900 sheets (704 in colour) of original costume designs, many with manuscript notes and cloth swatches; 104 photocopies (forty-eight in colour) of costume designs (60% with attached swatches); four sketchbooks of monochrome and colour designs; over 120 production photographs; and some sixty programs. The collection covers Corbett's career from the 1950s to 1995. [XZ 1 MS A158]

ERIC DONKIN COLLECTION. Biographical information, correspondence, photographs, reviews, programs, and other materials relating to the life and career of Eric Donkin (1929–1998), a well-known character actor born in Liverpool. Donkin played leads in many of the major houses across the country, including Neptune Theatre (*King Lear,* 1977), Centaur Theatre, the National Arts Centre, and the Lorraine Kimsa Theatre for the Young. He is most noted for his twenty-five-year association with Ontario's Stratford Festival. [XZ1 MS B007–B008]

TONY VAN BRIDGE COLLECTION. Articles and reviews, photographs, correspondence, and other memorabilia relating to the career of British-born actor and director Tony Van Bridge (1917–2004) who arrived in Canada in 1954. He performed extensively in television, radio, and at the Stratford Festival. He directed at Stratford and in theatres across the country. Van Bridge was well-known for his acting, especially his portrayal of Shakespeare's loveable Falstaff. [XZ1 MS B106]

In addition to these ten significant archival collections, there are major individual performances, commemorative theatre events, and artistic achievements that illustrate Shakespearean themes and works. Many Canadian theatres and playwrights have reinterpreted and adapted Shakespeare's works in the past thirty years. The process of reinterpretation and adaptation is a focal point for the Canadian Adaptations of Shakespeare Project (CASP), now the largest digital archive studying the Shakespeare effect from a particular national (read Canadian) perspective. CASP has relied extensively on the L.W. Conolly Theatre Archives and on Shakespearean resources that reflect both universal Shakespearean qualities and particular Canadian viewpoints or original adaptations derived from the world's greatest playwright. The essence of Shakespeare is present in various types of publications and artistic representations held by the library, which also possesses a small number of theatre props such as Yorick's skull, part of the Phoenix Theatre holdings.

A variety of library materials are not included in the Shakespeare—Made in Canada exhibition, although they can be referenced in Archival and Special Collections. For example, there are many house programs that not only serve as a record of a theatre's production, but also satisfy the need to inform audiences attending a given performance. Shakespeare's plays are well represented by many Ontario theatres, such as CentreStage, Theatre Passe Muraille, the Crest Theatre, the Grand Theatre (London, Ontario), Black Theatre Canada, Canadian Stage Theatre, and Toronto Free Theatre Archives. The Richard Rose Collection in particular is strong with performance scripts and includes class notes and essays for his teachings on Shakespeare at York University.

SET MODELS. The University of Guelph theatre archives house the largest collection of scale set models (or maquettes) for theatre in Canada. Over the years, the work highlighting Shakespearean productions by a number of designers, such as Cameron Porteous, has been preserved. The models serve the purpose of linking performance with stage sets and furnishings, and range from the ordinary to the elaborate depending on practical realities of theatrical budgets. In the Shakespeare—Made in Canada exhibition, there are four maquettes from our collection:

- *Twelfth Night* designed by Cameron Porteous for Citadel Theatre in 1998
- two productions of *Romeo and Juliet* designed by Jim Plaxton for Toronto Free Theatre in 1985 and 1986 (also known as *Dream in High Park,* this production is particularly noteworthy as it was designed for outdoor seasons in North York)
- *The Tempest* designed by William Chesney for Skylight Theatre in 1987

For more information about our collection of set models, please consult our library's theatre archive website <www.lib.uoguelph.ca/resources/archives/theatre/>.

POSTERS. Shakespeare advertised! The theatre archives hold many attractive and colourful posters. The Shakespeare—Made in Canada exhibition includes posters for *Hamlet* from the Phoenix Theatre's 1981 production and Theatre Passe Muraille's 1982 production. Also, Black Theatre Canada's *A Caribbean Midsummer Night's Dream* is an interesting 1983 adaptation that celebrated the company's tenth anniversary. Adapted from Shakespeare's original, the production was shortened and enriched by the sounds and sights of the Caribbean—its music, dances, costumes, speech rhythms, drumbeats. A mixed company of Black and white actors delivered Shakespeare's poetic prose with a distinctive Caribbean cadence.

TECHNICAL DRAWINGS. The technical aspect of staging a production in a finite space is illustrated by many drawings that bring a creative endeavour to life. The specifications for Toronto Free Theatre provide the details for layouts, set changes, and furnishings for *Romeo and Juliet* that reveal both the play development and the financial considerations of smaller theatres. Shakespeare's *Tempest* at the Skylight Theatre—Toronto's first professional outdoor theatre in North York—drawn by Canadian scenic artist William Chesney is another fine example of this type of work that the library holds, and is complemented by the displayed set model.

PRODUCTION PHOTOGRAPHS. Photographs can be used to visualize productions in different ways. Often, they serve to illustrate the realities performers or directors wish to capture, but they also may be used to establish information about the play, the time it was set in, or memorable stage events. Production photographs from many theatres, including Black Theatre Canada, the Grand Theatre in London, the NDWT (Ne'er-Do-Well-Thespians), and Stratford Festival, as well as those from the William Hutt collection, provide a fascinating visual record of Shakespeare in Canada.

COSTUME DESIGNS. The contributions of Canadian costume designers are represented by holdings from the Centre Stage Theatre Company, and from the William Hutt and Peter Blais collections. Blais has been involved in many aspects of Canadian theatre and has made contributions to productions across this country.

IN SUM, the L. W. Conolly Theatre Archives has emerged in the short span of two decades as a significant national resource for theatre studies with holdings that reflect on Canada's extraordinary relationship with Shakespeare, but also on Canadian theatrical culture more generally. With more than one hundred and twenty-five separate collections, it has become an essential repository for the study of Canadian theatre and continues to grow at a rapid pace.

Lorne Bruce is head of Archival and Special Collections at the University of Guelph Library and is engaged extensively with the acquisition, arrangement, and description of theatre collections for library users. He also has published articles and books in Canada, the United States, and Europe on a variety of library and book history topics ranging from ancient Rome to the public library system in Ontario.

Lorna Rourke is a University of Guelph liaison librarian who currently is developing collections and providing research assistance for students and faculty for English, Theatre Studies, Library Science, and the Bachelor of Arts and Sciences program. She is a recipient of the University of Guelph Faculty Association Academic Librarianship award and teaches a course on academic libraries through the Faculty of Information and Media Studies, University of Western Ontario in London.

JUDITH NASBY

Finding Shakespeare in Contemporary Portraiture

THE PORTRAIT GENRE has changed dramatically since the seventeenth century when the artist's objective was to make an accurate visual depiction of a person. Today portraits are idiosyncratic, evocative, and broadly open to interpretation by the artist and the viewer alike, rather than literal representations of people. This exhibition of contemporary portraiture presents works by artists from across Canada, revealing the influence of William Shakespeare on contemporary notions of character and serving as a counterpoint to the Sanders seventeenth-century oil-on-panel, considered to be the likeness of the Bard.

Shakespeare's characters show life as it is. They are as relevant today as they were to his Elizabethan and Jacobean audiences. Shakespeare has influenced our understanding of human frailty and passion through characters like Hamlet, Ophelia, Lear, and Falstaff, types we readily identify within the realm of our own life experiences. Who cannot recognize, in today's world, the overweight, drunken Falstaff: a dishonest braggart, who is somehow still appealing? Artist Verne Harrison's contemporary portrayal incorporates Falstaff's famous quotes: *"Sit on my knee, Doll"* [1]

LEFT Fiona Kinsella

(cake) Patron Saint of England (Feast Day of St. George, April 23rd. Protector against poison.)

Royal icing, pearls, teeth, dirt, seeds, horse hair, skin, silver, morning dew, cloth, armour, hair of a woman, molasses, cup, icon, wild rose, hemlock, hebenon, water, spirits, sword, cuff links, sleep, redpath, fondant icing.

Hamilton, Burlington, Guelph, New Brunswick, Prague, ?, ?, ?,

Verne Harrison,
*Henry the Fourth, Act II,
scene 4: "Sit on my knee, Doll,"*
2006 (digital photograph,
acrylic, oil, and varnish on
canvas)

as the title of the work, and "I am old..."[2] printed on his tee-shirt. Teenaged girls look on completely bored. Harrison says, "His lecherousness is fascinating to young people. He's worried that no one finds him interesting anymore, so he's always trying to create the myth of Falstaff." Harrison himself is a master of parody; here, he casts himself as the fallible character in a way that troubles facile depictions of Falstaff as a lovable troublemaker.

Painter Shannon Reynolds is role-playing as well—as a stage director in *Dramatis Personae* (2005), her series of stock theatrical character portraits in oil. For this project, she invited stage actors to mimic archetypal character roles: heroes, villains, crones, sages, fools, coquettes, and femmes fatales. In each portrait, she created a tableau with props and encouraged the model to dress for the part. "I was heartened by the idea that an actor could succeed by simply assuming the posture, dress, and mannerisms of the character without profound psychological insight into the role, and through mere imitation would become the character."[3] The sitters' direct gaze creates a compelling bond with the audience, traversing the artist's frame and the actor's stage. Reynolds' objective is to marry literary influences to ideas about painted portraiture. To enhance the literary underpinnings of each character, she incorporates text scratched and worked into the birch panels. Reynolds explains that "a very patient viewer could piece all the words together."[4] For *The Coquette,* she integrates excerpts from Henry James's *Daisy Miller* with flirting tips culled from Internet sites; *The Lusty Woman*'s text is an extract of *The Wife of Bath's Prologue* from Chaucer's *Canterbury Tales.*

Jaclyn Conley's painting *Graces* (2004) is a contemporized version of the enduring classical theme of the three nymphs, representing the virtues of beauty, mirth, and cheer. The virtues are heavily eulogized in Shakespeare's sonnets, in which he propounds themes of love and beauty; however, the sonnets are also laced with criticisms of the frivolity and ephemerality of youth. Conley presents a post-feminist questioning of feminine beauty by painting the nubile female form for the scrutiny of the female gaze, her subjects mimicking the gestures of bathing suit models found in mail order catalogues.

First published in 1577, Raphael Holinshed's *Chronicles of England, Scotland and Ireland* is acknowledged as the source of the plot of *Macbeth*. Shakespeare reimagines Holinshed's nymph-like sisters as demonic supernatural witches, a dark mirroring of the enchanted fairies.[5] In seventeenth-century England, witchcraft was considered a very real threat to a person's well-being, in contrast to contemporary interpretations of witchcraft, known as Wicca or the Old Religion. FASTWÜRMS, the shared authorship of artists Dai Skuse and Kim Kozzi, incorporate Wiccan symbolism into their work. The use of pentagrams and horned composite creatures in their life-sized self-portrait, titled *Wurmhole, Crew Portrait #2 (Security & Horticulture)* (1994), reveals this connection. In the photograph, the artists present themselves in Wiccan regalia with scythes, cat familiars, and moonbeams for nocturnal journeying. They cast themselves in the role of spaceship security officers and gardeners, responsible for nurturing positive growth and for pruning anti-social behaviour. Their hypnotized expressions suggest the power of the spell. *Wurmhole, Crew Portrait #2 (Security & Horticulture)* is from FASTWÜRMS' exhibition WURMHOLE, a room-sized installation created for the Koffler Gallery, North York, in 1994. The entire installation was conceived as a flight deck for a witch's spaceship stylized after the high modernist décor of early *Star Trek* episodes, a parody of Gene Roddenberry's popular television program, which frequently made use of Shakespearean allusion. FASTWÜRMS' work references tropes of witchcraft that originated in Shakespeare's time.

Shannon Reynolds,
The Lusty Woman, 2005
(oil on birch panel)

Stephen Livick's *Hijra with Black Bindi* and *Costumed Hijra* (both 1987) are part of a larger series of gum bichromate prints exploring the cultural fabric of Calcutta's inner city. Livick used an unwieldy large box camera to make street portraits illuminated by intense sunlight. This complicated nineteenth-century process, also known as photo aquatint, produces exquisitely coloured prints, a perfect medium for depicting the splendour of the saris and jewels and the heightened level of theatricality and performativity governing the daily lives of Livick's subjects.

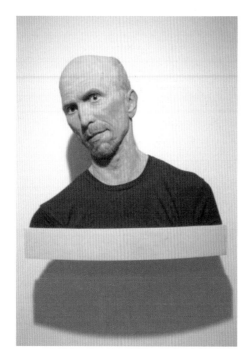 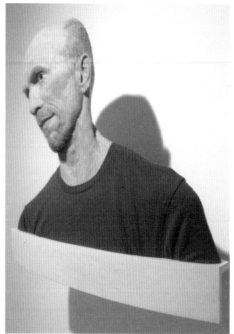

130

His images are remarkable for their intensity and for the emotional bond he attained with his subjects, allowing them to reveal the fragility and the vulnerability of their existence. *Hijra* is a Hindi term describing the "third sex," the male-to-female, transgendered, and intersexed persons in the culture of the Indian subcontinent. The culture and identity of *hijra* is an ancient and accepted part of Indian culture. Livick's portraits evoke complex questions of gender and of how the gaze of the subject mediates cultural difference. Is the lesson to be learned from Livick's *Hijras* comparable to what Shakespeare's plays teach us about gendered identities and performativity through both the characters who cross-dress and the actors of his day, all male, who played female roles?

Evan Penny questions our idea of what is real in his *Self-Portrait* (2003) made from silicone, pigment, hair, and fabric. This extraordinarily "realistic" object reinforces representation as a construct. The anamorphic, skewed portrait, which appears life-like from a frontal perspective and dramatically distorted from an oblique angle, challenges the nature of "looking" and our ability to interpret reality. In the time of Shakespeare, artists experimented with anamorphism, the mathematical distortion of an image that is visually incomprehensible from one perspective, yet clearly visible from another. Penny's *Self-Portrait* leads us to question how any portrait can be a true likeness since it is always based on an artist's construction of the image (and affected by technique, medium, aesthetics, philosophy, cultural context, and so forth). The question of how an original image is mediated by and through the artist's envisioning is worth bearing in mind anytime a viewer observes a portrait.

Hollywood mythologizing is introduced into the exhibition with Andrew Harwood's *Flower Rider* (2006), a digitized photograph that depicts Peter Fonda in the 1969 film *Easy Rider*. Bedecked with sequins, this image is from Harwood's ongoing series exploring transportation and the "subversion of pop culture masculine identities." [6] The easy rider fancies himself introspective and psychologically complex, a seeker of truth and a breaker of convention. Harwood's easy rider is an urban nomad, as flippant in his affectations as Shakespeare's Hamlet is to Ophelia, who waits in vain for the prince to show her signs of affection.

Stephen Livick, *Hijra in Black Bindi* and *Costumed Hjira*, both 1987 (gum bichromate)

Evan Penny, *Self-Portrait* (frontal and oblique views), 2003 (silicone, pigment, hair, fabric)

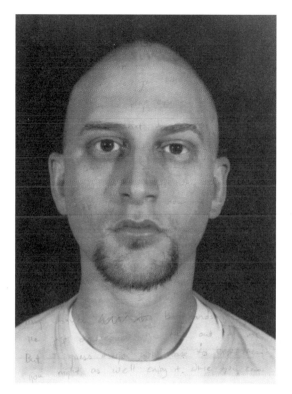 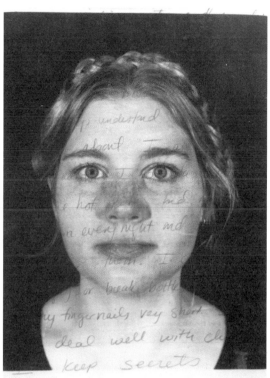

Jean-Paul Tousignant,
Nathan, 2002 and *Erin*, 2003
(both liquid photo emulsion
and graphite on Arches)

RIGHT Cheryl Ruddock,
Recovered Kelp, Lost Dress,
2006 (mixed media on Japanese
gampi paper)

The vulnerability expressed in Jean-Paul Tousignant's portraits *Nathan* (2002) and *Erin* (2003) is reflected in the sitters' eyes, which engage the viewer; their quotidian jottings scrawled across the surface of the photographs are like a page from a diary. The pairing of *Nathan* and *Erin* is filled with sensuous tension, suggestive of a more complicated relationship: Shakespeare's young lovers Romeo and Juliet.

Recovered Kelp, Lost Dress (2006), Cheryl Ruddock's two-metre long drawing on diaphanous Japanese gampi paper, recalls Shakespeare's Ophelia. Ruddock's hand-stitched drawing of a dress caught among kelp fronds and seed pods is tissue-like as it hangs on the wall, the transparency of its surface like a lake in the thin light of day. "Everything is there but the body. The work is about our lives, finding something horrible or tender in the water is what we live with everyday."[7] Ruddock uses touches of red, suggestive of Ophelia's suicide.

Mohawk artist Shelly Niro takes a poetic approach to personal history in *Ghost* (2005): "People pass and become mythologized. They become ghost-like and paths for the oral history of a family, a community, and a country. The man is the embodiment of the spirits."[8] The man

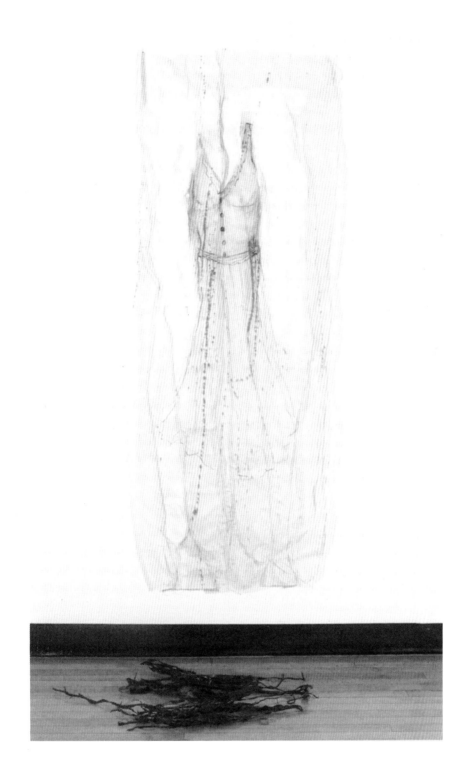

Oswaldo DeLeón Kantule,
*La Mujer de Agua en su
Hamaca de Esmeraldas (or The
Water Woman in her Emerald
Hammock)*, 2006
(acrylic on canvas)

Mary Aski-Piyesiwiskwew
Longman, *Elk Man Waiting For
Love*, 1996
(Matrix G, elk antlers,
CD soundtrack)

depicted in *Ghost* is in a dream state, with his psychic double hovering at his shoulder. This mysterious image is from the series *Ghosts, Girls, and Grandmas* (2005), in which Niro explores storytelling and mythmaking through portraiture that includes images of her mother and daughter, together with images of rocks and trees that appear to have their own transformational presence. For Niro, *Ghost* is a signifier of sacred Iroquois stories and ancient histories that are forever fluid in their telling and beyond written definition in a Western sense. This boundless narrative energy perhaps links Shakespearean storytelling in all its adaptive signifying richness to other storytelling traditions, equally rich and suggestive. Niro uses a frame made from wampum, comprising belts of dark and light shells, as a significant cultural reference symbolizing the Iroquois community. In so doing, she extends the traditional purpose of wampum as a healing conduit, as a symbolic agreement between nations, and as an historical record representing the continuation and vitality of Iroquois culture.

Kuna artist Oswaldo DeLeón Kantule, who was born in Ustupu, Kuna Yala, Panama, and is now based in London, Ontario, also draws on his traditional religion and mythology to create powerful contemporary statements about life, death, and societal and environmental concerns. "I use the ancestral symbolism of my people, present in our daily lives as an intimate language of communication between myself, my work, and the observer."[9] His painting *La Mujer de Agua en su Hamaca de Esmeraldas* (or *The Water Woman in her Emerald Hammock*) (2006) is a profound expression of the intimate and essential linkage between humans and nature. The female progenitor in his painting is at once the tree of life and the blood of the earth, as her veins unite with the sea. Kantule's figure can be likened to Shakespeare's wood sprites that appear in forest scenes, often at night and by moonlight. The characters of Puck, Oberon, and Titania from *A Midsummer Night's Dream* are forest fairies, both miraculous and mad, who yield transformative powers.

Saulteau artist Mary Aski-Piyesiwiskwew Longman presents a contemporary depiction of an ancient Plains story in her sculpture, *Elk Man Waiting for Love* (1996). Longman, who is a member of the Gordon First Nation located near Punnichy, Saskatchewan, explains that "First Nation stories communicate the experience of life and metaphors of life, and it is within these stories that we learn the history and lessons

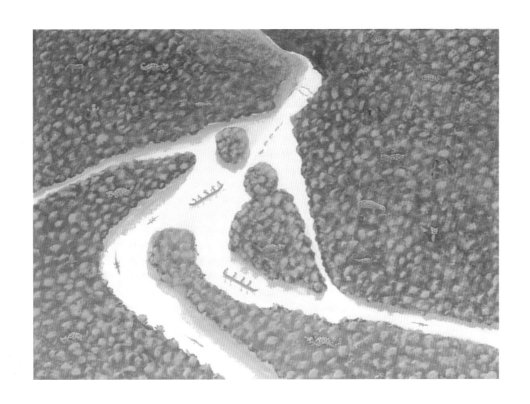

This present *Monday*, being the 23d of *MAY*,
Will be presented a TRAGEDY, call'd

ROMEO and JULIET.

Romeo by Mr BARRY
Capulet by Mr SPARKS
Montague by Mr. R____ AN
Escalus by Mr. ANDERSON, ____ Pa____ ____HITE.
Benvolio by Mr. GIBSON, ____ La____ ____BARRINGTON.
Fryar *Laurence* by M____ ____OUT,
Tibalt by Mr. C____ ____NG.
Gregory by Mr BENNET, ____ Abram by Mr. DUNSTALL.
Sampson by Mr. COLLINS, ____ Balthazar by Mr.
Mercutio by Mr. DYER
Nurse by Mrs. PITT,

Juliet by Miss NOSSITER.

With a *MINUET*
By Mr. POITIER and Mad CAPDEVILLE
And a MASQUERADE DANCE
proper to the PLAY.

An Additional Scene *will* be introduc'd, rep
The Funeral Procession of *JULIET*
Which will be accompanied with
A SOLEMN DIRGE
The Vocal Parts by Mr. Hreard. Mr. Legg Mr. Baker. Mr. Roberts,
Mrs. Lampe, Mrs. Chambers. Miss Young, and Others.
To which will be added a Pantomime Entertainment, call'd

HARLEQUIN SORCERER:

136

of life and learn to make meaning of life itself." [10] In her sculpture, a
kneeling young man sprouts the head and antlers of an elk. The elk
man holds two stones intertwined with the tresses of his desired love.
"He hopes his love medicine will entice her to accept his love. Out of
his mouth is the powerful sound of the elk calling with urgency and
longing." [11] The baying is audible by means of a hidden audiotape. In
this work, Longman depicts a Plains courting ritual creating a poignant
image of unrequited love. This image at once references the sorrowful,
star-crossed lovers from *Romeo and Juliet,* and the magical transformation of Nick Bottom as he metamorphoses from man into animal in *A
Midsummer Night's Dream.*

Bottom, an Athenian weaver and one of Shakespeare's greatest comic
figures, fancies himself irresistible to women, even when Puck mi-
raculously transforms his head into that of an ass without his knowledge. In his obliviousness, Bottom thinks that the fairy princess Titania
is madly in love with him. In one scene, Puck sprinkles a love potion
over Titania's eyelids and she believes herself to be in love with the ass-
headed Bottom. Artist Ryan Price has created an extraordinary *Bottom
Head,* a theatrical mask of a donkey's head, displayed in the Possible
Worlds installation curated by Pat Flood. This eerie, wearable mask
deflates pomposity and challenges any reductive assumptions about
human nature. Which, after all, is the mask: the human face or the
animal face?

In *The Hobby Horse,* Montreal artist Lyne Lapointe creates a portrait
of Shakespeare as a child's toy hobby horse, a stuffed horse's head at the
end of a long stick. The framed miniature portrait is mounted on a large
production poster that, in Old English, announces the cast of *Romeo
and Juliet,* each letter meticulously hand painted by Lapointe to appear
aged and worn. Lapointe identifies the hobby horse as a contemporary symbol of gay culture, as she is interested in the proposition that
Shakespeare may have been homosexual. In Shakespeare's early sonnets,
he writes about his great love of a young man, exemplified by "Shall I
compare thee to a summer's day?" [12]—arguably the best known and
most admired of his 154 poems. It was not uncommon in Shakespeare's
time for men to demonstrate deep affection for other men, and the
Bard's use of gender-switching, such as in *Twelfth Night,* is well-docu-
mented. The linguistic term "hobby horse" is found in Shakespeare's
texts, but for other purposes that belie the origin of our modern usage

Lyne Lapointe,
The Hobby Horse, 2006
(wood, paper, oil paint, metal,
pearl, printed photograph)

137

Susan Bozic, *Invitation*, 2003
(silver print photograph)

of the word: as a reference to long-lost folk culture in *Hamlet*, "For, O, for O, the hobby-horse is forgot"[13]; and to obsessive behaviour in *Love's Labour's Lost*, "Callest thou my love 'hobby-horse'?"[14]

In her decadent still-life photograph titled *Invitation* (2003), Susan Bozic creates a tableau at the centre of which is a great black bear surrounded by props and drapery as if on a proscenium stage, the curtain opened to reveal the bear at sup. We are unsure whether the image is a taxidermist's tour-de-force or a live bear with its paws elegantly placed on soup bowls. Bozic conflates the animal image as a trophy rug elevated to the head of the table with the bear as a potential endangered species honoured with a celebratory feast. Her portrait of the bear as dinner host is in sharp contrast to Shakespearean times when bear-baiting was as much popular entertainment as were Shakespeare's plays at the Globe Theatre in London.

Animal references are also found in Fiona Kinsella's sculpture titled (*cake*) *Patron Saint of England* (*Feast Day of St. George, April 23rd. Protector against poison.*) (2006). Kinsella's cake is displayed on an upholstered base in celebration of April 23, the feast day of St. George. "During the past year, I have been working on a series of cakes referencing religious relics and the phenomenon of the incorruptible bodies of the saints.

In making this artwork, I was struck by the discrete parallels between St. George and William Shakespeare." [15] Shakespeare was born on April 23, 1564, and died on April 23, 1616. By the fifteenth century, St. George's Day was as important as Christmas Day. The saint's popularity, based on his mythical profile as a dragon slayer, continues to present times as he is the patron saint of both England and Canada. (Incidentally, the city of Guelph was founded on St. George's Day in 1827 by the novelist John Galt.) Kinsella's intriguing visual metaphors link St. George, as a protector against poisons, to Shakespeare's play *Hamlet*: "this pearl is thine" [16]—the cup of poison that was the cause of Gertrude's demise. The jaws in the artwork represent the dragon and the fondant roses signify the wild rose, the English symbol for the feast day. Kinsella's relic cake is a rich metaphor linking St. George to England, to Shakespeare, to Canada, and, in a way quite unintended, to Guelph.

The artists selected for this exhibition extend our ideas of what constitutes a portrait with evocative and intriguing works that explore characterization and human nature, while also commenting on social and environmental issues. They do so in ways that reference Shakespeare —sometimes unconsciously. They also engage us with how portraiture provides an important medium for articulating issues of identity, and how that identity is constructed through the narrative of the portrait as both a historical and an allegorical object. Their metaphorically rich literary and historical references engage us in an ongoing enquiry into the role of portraiture in contemporary visual culture.

Fiona Kinsella

(cake) Patron Saint of England (Feast Day of St. George, April 23rd. Protector against poison.)

Royal icing, pearls, teeth, dirt, seeds, horse hair, skin, silver, morning dew, cloth, armour, hair of a woman, molasses, cup, icon, wild rose, hemlock, hebenon, water, spirits, sword, cuff links, sleep, redpath, fondant icing.

Hamilton, Burlington, Guelph, New Brunswick, Prague, ?, ?, ?,

ENDNOTES

1 William Shakespeare, *The Second Part of King Henry VI,* ed. Norman N. Holland and Sylvan Barnet (New York: The New American Library, 1965), 93, 6.2.231. References are to act, scene, and line.

2 William Shakespeare. *The Second Part of King Henry VI,* ed. Norman N. Holland and Sylvan Barnet (New York: The New American Library, 1965), 95, 6.2.278. References are to act, scene, and line.

3 "The Play's the Thing: Confessions from Behind the Scenes," *The New Quarterly: Canadian Writers & Writing* 95 (Summer 2005): 159.

4 Derek Weiler, "Director's Cut: A Conversation with Shannon Reynolds." *The New Quarterly: Canadian Writers & Writing* 95 (Summer 2005): 175.

5 Amanda Mabillard, "An Analysis of Shakespeare's Sources for *Macbeth*," *Shakespeare Online* (2000), http://www.shakespeare-online.com/playanalysis/macbethsources.html (accessed November 29, 2006).

6 Paul Petro Contemporary Art, "Trucker," (2004), http://www.paulpetro.com/harwood/2004.shtml (accessed September 28, 2006).

7 Judith Nasby, interview with the artist, 2006.

8 Judith Nasby, interview with the artist, 2006.

9 Oswaldo DeLeón Kantule, "Artist's Statement," http://deleonkantule.tripod.com/statement.htm (accessed March 19, 2006).

10 Mary Longman, "Autobiographical Statement," http://www.marylongman.com/statement.html (accessed June 12, 2006).

11 Patricia Deadman, *Mary Aski-Piyesiwiskwew Longman* (Regina: Mackenzie Art Gallery, 2005), 35.

12 Amanda Mabillard, "An Analysis of Shakespeare's Sonnet 18," *Shakespeare Online* (2000), http://www.shakespeare-online.com/sonnets/18detail.html (accessed December 7, 2006).

13 William Shakespeare. *Hamlet, in Four Tragedies,* ed. David Bevington, et al. (New York: Bantam Books, 1988), 97, 3.2.133. References arc to act, scene, and line.

14 William Shakespeare, *Love's Labour's Lost,* ed. Richard David, et el. (London: Methuen Co. Ltd., 1966), Page, 3.1.29. References are to act, scene, and line.

15 Judith Nasby, correspondence with the artist, 2006.

16 William Shakespeare, *Four Tragedies,* ed. David Bevington (New York: Bantam Books, 1988), 167, 5.2.283. References are to act, scene, and line.

Judith Nasby is director and curator of Macdonald Stewart Centre and adjunct professor in the School of Fine Art and Music at the University of Guelph. She has published over fifty publications including *Irene Avaalaaqiaq: Myth and Reality* and *Rolph Scarlett: Painter, Designer, Jeweller,* both McGill Queen's University Press.

| *JIM HUNT*

Anamorphic Art in the Time of Shakespeare

For sorrow's eye, glazed with blinding tears,
Divides one thing entire to many objects;
Like perspectives, which rightly gaz'd upon,
Show nothing but confusion, ey'd awry,
Distinguish form.
Richard II, Act II, scene 2

Jim Hunt discusses the invention of anamorphism in the time of Shakespeare and its many applications in art, science, and mathematics from the sixteenth century to present day. For the Learning Comons in the Shakespeare—Made in Canada exhibition, Hunt created an installation of anamorphic displays that deconstruct the complexities of the practice.

WHEN FILIPPO BRUNELLESCHI (1377–1446) invented and mathematically described the artistic technique of geometrical perspective, he revolutionized painting, allowing for the naturalistic representation of single unified scenes to develop. Anamorphism—the study of distorted projections or drawings that become visible when viewed from a particular perspective or with a special mirror—was a natural outgrowth of this intense interest in visual perspective. The scientist-artists of the period—for example, Leonardo da Vinci (1452–1519) and Albrecht Dürer (1471–1528)—attempted to apply mathematical and physical principles to the art of perspective, considering cases of extreme perspective (optic anamorphosis) and distortions produced by reflection in mirrors of various forms (dioptric anamorphosis).

A bike lane indicator

RIGHT Hans Holbein,
The Ambassadors, 1533
(oil on oak) with a digital
reconstruction of the skull
image below

Anamorphic art was a popular form of both serious art and visual entertainment beginning in the sixteenth century. While its methods and geometrical elucidation belong to the seventeenth century, it was most practiced as a serious art form in the eighteenth century, one that often used anamorphism to manipulate an image so that the true message, often political in nature, was readable only by the initiated. By the nineteenth century, it was almost completely relegated to the nursery as an amusement for children. Nevertheless, it retains some popularity today, and a small coterie of artists still practice it.

The earliest known anamorphoses were those of da Vinci and took the form of a laterally stretched child's face and a sketch of an eye. Today anamorphoses are actually commonplace in busy cities. The traffic directions and symbols that are painted on roadways are distorted anamorphically. Consider a common bicycle lane indicator: the upper figure is what is actually painted on the pavement, while the lower is what a driver sees from about three metres away. The typical form of anamorphic display seen today requires reflection in a mirror for reconstruction of the image. Of the possible types of display, the cylindrical mirror is the most common.

Treatises on the mathematics of perspective and anamorphism were produced, particularly in the seventeenth century. In that prime period of development, much of the analysis of anamorphic perspective was done using the language of geometry. Today researchers continue that form of analysis. It is only natural to do so as geometrical methods are certain to provide instant and insightful information about phenomena related to anamorphism. The introduction of the high-speed computer, however, has stimulated interest in exact analytical solutions to the various types of anamorphic transformation. In some cases, the analytical solutions are simple to the point of triviality and have been known for a long time. An example of a "trivial" solution is the mathematics for the plane anamorphosis (as in the bicycle lane indicator) viewed from infinity; an example of a "simple" solution is the analysis of the same bicycle lane indicator as viewed from a finite distance. Some solutions, like those for an anamorphosis formed in a convex cylindrical mirror, are neither obvious nor simple. Many of these have only recently been derived, most particularly through work done at the University of Guelph Physics department.

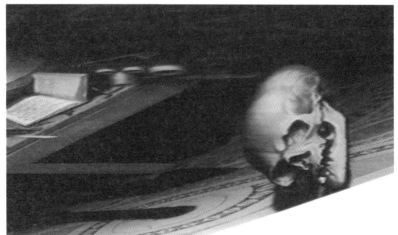

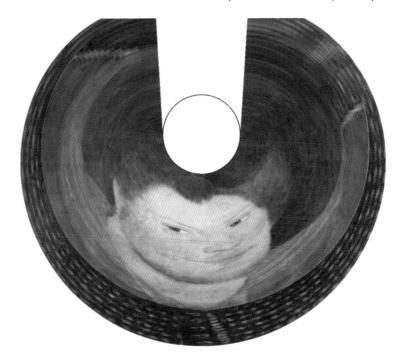

An anamorphic rendering of the Sanders portrait created by Jim Hunt. A cylindrical mirror placed at the centre will yield an inverted reconstruction of the image in its reflection.

The immediate fruit of this type of analysis is the ability to apply the transformations to any digitized image. Using analytic expressions for the "transforms" and the power of the modern computer, it is now possible to undertake analyses of works of anamorphic art such as the famous "skull" in Hans Holbein's *The Ambassadors* (1533). Such analyses can yield important information. For example, a photograph of *The Ambassadors* taken before its restoration in 1996 can be compared to a photograph of the painting as it is today, after the restoration. By using the same electronic calculation, the two can be compared to see if the restorers have been faithful to Holbein's original.

This and other graphics of historical interest can be examined using exact mathematical analysis and the digital computer. The Shakespeare—Made in Canada Learning Commons demonstrates some of these possibilities in a non-mathematical way.

Jim Hunt is professor emeritus in the physics department at the University of Guelph.

144

Credits

Pg 60   Collection of Astrid Janson

Pg 73   Collection of David Gardner;
        Photo: Lutz Dille

Pg 74   *top* Canadian Theatre Museum
        994.1.199.F; *bottom* Collection
        of Sandra and Samuel Esses,
        courtesy of the Macdonald
        Stewart Art Centre; Photo:
        Exhibitions International

Pg 75   Stratford Festival of Canada

Pg 76   Collection of Charlotte Dean

Pg 77   Collection of Charlotte Dean

Pg 78   Collection of Dr. Jules and
        Mrs. Jo Harris

Pg 79   L. W. Conolly Theatre Archives,
        University of Guelph, Photo:
        C. Porteous

Pg 80–81   Collection of Dany Lyne

Pg 82   Collection of Teresa Przybylski

Pg 83   Collection of Susan Benson

Pg 85   Stratford Festival of Canada

Pg 88–89   Collection of Sorouja Moll

Pg 96   Collection/Photo: Yves Renaud

Pg 99   Collection of Charles Bolster

Pg 100   Collection of Charles Bolster

Pg 102   Collection of Hélène
        Stevenson; Photo: Robert
        Gurik

Pg 103   Collection/Photo: Daniel
        Kieffer

Pg 106   Canadian Adaptations of
        Shakespeare Project Archives

Pg 107   Collection/Photo: Tibor
        Egervari

Pg 108   Collection of Leanore Lieblein

Pg 110   Native Earth Performing Arts;
        Photo: Nina Lee Aquino

Pg 114   Photos: Marion Gruner and
        Sorouja Moll

Pg 118   L. W. Conolly Theatre Archives,
        University of Guelph

Pg 127   Collection of Fiona Kinsella

Pg 128   Collection of Verne Harrison

Pg 129   Collection of Shannon
        Reynolds

Pg 130   *top* Collection of William R.
        and Sydney Pieschel, Calgary,
        courtesy of the TrépanierBaer
        Gallery, Calgary; *bottom* Gift of
        Ron and Shari Silverstein, 1993,
        Macdonald Stewart Art Centre
        MS993.009 / MS993.012

Pg 132   Purchased with funds raised
        by the Art Centre Volunteers
        and with financial support
        from the Canada Council for
        the Arts Acquisition Assistance
        Program, 2006, Macdonald
        Stewart Art Centre 7549 / 7550

Pg 133   Collection of Cheryl Ruddock

Pg 135   *top* Collection of Oswaldo
        DeLeón Kantule; *bottom*
        Thunder Bay Art Gallery,
        Purchased with the support
        of the Canada Council for the
        Arts Acquisition Assistance
        Program and funding from the
        Walter and Duncan Gordon
        Foundation

Pg 136   Purchased with funds raised
        by the Art Centre Volunteers
        and with financial support
        from the Canada Council for
        the Arts Acquisition Assistance
        Program, 2006, Macdonald
        Stewart Art Centre 7844

Pg 138   Collection of Susan Bozic

Pg 139   Collection of Fiona Kinsella

Pg 143   © The National Gallery,
        London (Bought 1890)

Pg 144   Jim Hunt

Our Sponsors

Oberon Sponsor

City of Guelph

Puck Sponsors

AT THE GUELPH COMMUNITY FOUNDATION

BMO Bank of Montreal

Peaseblossom Sponsors

Dr. Scott Griffin   Dr. W.C. Winegard

The Rotary Club of Guelph

The Rotary Club of Guelph Charitable Foundation

A Better Place For You

CHARTERED ACCOUNTANTS

John Bligh & Nancy Bailey Bligh

Thisbe Sponsors

Mote Sponsors

Sue Bennett   Holody Family   Jane & Richard Dell

Jacqueline Murray

Balnar Management

Linamar

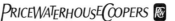 

i'm lovin' it

zehrs

Festival Sponsors

Chris Vandergrift   Dr. Janet Wardlaw   Hal & Nancy Jackson

Mr. & Mrs. Doug Bridge

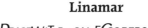

THERAPY PARTNERS INC.

Guelph Wellington Men's Club

Mr. Aubrey Hagar   Joanne Coyle   Bob Hammond

About the typeface

This book is set in Cartier Book, type designer Rod McDonald's sensitive revival of Cartier, the first Canadian text typeface. Created by celebrated designer and typographer Carl Dair, Cartier was commissioned by the Canadian government and released in 1967 to celebrate Canada's centennial. Retaining the distinctive energy of Dair's original design, McDonald has refined the letterforms specifically for text setting, while also expanding the face into a fully functional type family. Cartier Book is an elegant, functional, and highly readable face.

Library and Archives Canada
Cataloguing in Publication

Shakespeare—made in Canada :
contemporary Canadian adaptations
in theatre, pop media and visual arts /
co-editors: Daniel Fischlin + Judith
Nasby ; exhibition curators: Daniel
Fischlin + Judith Nasby ; exhibition
co-curators: Lorne Bruce ... [et al.].

Catalogue of an exhibition at the
Macdonald Stewart Art Centre,
Guelph, Ont., on January 11 - June 10,
2007.

ISBN 0-920810-80-2

1. Shakespeare, William, 1564–1616—
Adaptations—Exhibitions.
2. Shakespeare, William, 1564–1616—
Illustrations—Exhibitions. 3. Arts,
Canadian—21st century—Exhibitions.
I. Fischlin, Daniel, 1957–
II. Nasby, Judith, 1945– III. Macdonald
Stewart Art Centre.

PR2883.S53 2007   704.9'498223307471343   C2006-906759-7

© 2007
Macdonald Stewart Art Centre
358 Gordon Street
Guelph, Ontario, Canada N1G 1Y1
TEL (519) 837-0010   FAX (519) 767-2661
info@msac.ca   www.msac.ca

Exhibition Shakespeare—Made in
    Canada: Contemporary Canadian
    Adaptations in Theatre, Pop Media
    and Visual Arts
Venue Macdonald Stewart Art Centre
    January 11 – June 10, 2007

Exhibition Curators Daniel Fischlin and
    Judith Nasby
Exhibition Co-curators Lorne Bruce, Jane
    Edmonds, Pat Flood, Jim Hunt,
    Leanore Lieblein, Richard Louttet,
    Diane Nalini de Kerckhove, Petra
    Schennach
Assistant Curator Dawn Owen
Publication Co-editors Daniel Fischlin
    and Judith Nasby
Design Kathe Gray / electric pear
Printing: Barney Printing Limited

*The Macdonald Stewart Art Centre (*MSAC*) is a public art gallery and sculpture park serving
Guelph and the surrounding region. MSAC was established in 1978 through a provincial act
as a not-for-profit corporation with four official sponsors: the City of Guelph, the County of
Wellington, the University of Guelph, and the Upper Grand District School Board.*

The cover and text pages of this exhibition catalogue are printed on Mohawk Options,
which contains 30% postconsumer waste fibre and is manufactured with windpower.